Getting Rich In Your Underwear
How To Start And Run A Profitable Home-Based Business

Peter Hupalo

Library of Congress Control Number: 2005922669

ISBN 0967162483

Book cover design by Jamon Walker of Mythic Design Studio (mythicstudio.com).

Printed in the United States of America

HCM Publishing
hcmpublishing.com

This publication is designed to provide information in regard to the subject matter covered. It is sold with the understanding that the publisher and the author are not engaged to render legal, accounting, or other professional services. If legal advice or other expert assistance is required, the services of a competent professional should be sought.

Table Of Contents

Chapter 1
Business Models
And
The Home Business

Welcome! I'm glad you purchased *Getting Rich In Your Underwear: How To Start And Run A Profitable Home-Based Business*. This book will help you get started in planning, setting up, and running your own home-based business. I also give you some guidance about personal financial planning to maximize the financial benefits of your business.

This book assumes you are new to running a business. The goal of *Getting Rich In Your Underwear: How To Start And Run A Profitable Home-Based Business* is to take you up to the point where you'll have enough information to successfully operate your own home-based business venture.

Home-based business ventures are ideal for part-time businesses. They are also well-suited to those who want to start a business on limited capital or those who want to adjust their business to their personal lifestyle.

Operating part-time and starting on limited funds are related. The advantage of a part-time startup is that a person can continue with traditional employment while building up the business. That gives the business time to establish itself and grow. It also gives the entrepreneur time to learn about the chosen business endeavor and adjust the company's business model as necessary before the business must become sufficiently profitable to support the entrepreneur. The value of the time before your business must become self-supporting can't be overemphasized.

Suppose you quit your day job and start a small business full-time. Let's also assume you have no other major sources of income. You probably have many monthly expenses that must be paid, such as rent or house payments, medical insurance, groceries, car insurance, entertainment, etc. Adding up those living expenses, you might find you need to earn $45,000 per year just to stay afloat.

Exercise: Calculate your monthly living expenses. Break down your expenses by categories, such as groceries, car repair, utilities, health insurance, dining, and entertainment. Each person's categories will differ. Use your bank statements to help with your estimates. Organize your expenses in a simple chart, like this:

$xx.xx	Groceries
$xx.xx	House Payment
$xx.xx	Health Insurance
$xx.xx	Car Payment
$xx.xx	Water Utility
$xx.xx	Gas/Electric Utilities
$xx.xx	Miscellaneous Expenses
—	
$xx.xx	Total Monthly Expenses

Expenses that are paid every month, such as a house payment, are easiest to record. For expenses that are paid quarterly, semiannually, or yearly, such as a semiannual house insurance payment, amortize the amount it costs per month. For example, if you pay $600 every six months for house insurance, the monthly amount is $100.

For expenses that vary from month to month, such as groceries, it's useful to average several months data together to get the approximate monthly expense. Suppose over the past twelve months, on groceries, you spent:

January:	$500
February:	$300
March:	$600
April:	$400
May:	$600
June:	$300
July:	$400
August	$900
September	$200
October	$300
November	$400
December	$500

Yearly Grocery Total: $5,400
Monthly Average: $5,400/12 = $450

We see that $450 per month on groceries is the appropriate amount to include in our budget. It's also handy to go over your monthly expense list and see what items can be reduced or eliminated. For example, if you spend $200 per month on lottery tickets, you probably could reduce or cut that. You might want to draw up another budget that represents your *absolute minimum expenses*. Just cut down on discretionary spending to arrive at that budget. That amount represents the absolute minimum amount of annual income you need to survive.

Consider purchasing a computer program, such as Quicken, to help you track your finances. At the very least, a calculator is necessary for averaging. Entering actual financial data for a number of years will give you the clearest picture of your spending.

You might wonder why it's so important to draw up a household budget or monitor your household expenses. When running a home-based business, you won't have an accounting staff to keep your books. It will be crucial to become familiar with the basics of financial management. If you've never evaluated your personal expenditures, you'll be at a disadvantage when starting your business. You need to learn to think in terms of numbers. Your personal finances are often the best place to start learning about financial and business management.

Further, income from home-based businesses is often erratic. It's important to know how much you personally spend each month to be sure your company is earning enough to make you financially comfortable.

To Do:

Purchase a calculator.
Purchase Quicken or another personal financial tracking program and learn to use it.

If your company takes two years before it becomes sufficiently profitable to support your personal lifestyle, you might burn through $90,000. Even if you had $90,000 saved, it probably wouldn't be prudent to spend your savings on living expenses while starting a home-based business.

Suppose you're thirty years old and plan to retire at age sixty. If you kept $90,000 invested for thirty years, at a ten-percent return, that amount would grow into about $1.5 million. That's a large future amount to risk to start your home-based business. I mention this, because many younger people contemplate dipping into 401(k) savings or other retirement savings to start a home-based business. Unfortunately, many find that after a year or two their business isn't earning much money and their retirement nest egg is depleted. This is why I suggest starting part-time.

Once you find your small business can support your living expenses, it's easier to move toward complete self-employment, if that's your choice. I encourage new entrepreneurs to invest time, rather than money, when possible, when starting a new business. Consider the time spent learning about business as an investment in your future.

Many home-based businesses are operated part-time over many years and provide the entrepreneur with extra income while the entrepreneur maintains traditional employment. Such businesses are often run during weekends. And, the entrepreneur never decides to cease traditional employment.

Suppose, working weekends, you earn a modest $30,000 per year in your part-time, home-based business. After taxes, suppose you keep $20,000 of that. If you were to invest the $20,000 each year and you were to get a 10% return on your annual investment, you'd have over a million dollars in twenty years.

To minimize taxes, you could save about half of this money in tax-deferred retirement accounts, such as an SEP-IRA combined with a Roth IRA. The other half could be invested in mutual funds or stocks that tend to appreciate without generating a lot of taxable dividends. These would be quality investments you could hold for a long time. That way nearly all of your annual gains from investment would be sheltered from taxes.

While working twenty years to save a million dollars might not seem like such a tremendous achievement when you read about dot.com millionaires who become worth $50 million in three short years, it's a respectable gain and it's more easily achievable.

To put things into perspective, consider that, according to the Census Bureau, the average high-school graduate earns a total of about $1.2 million dollars in a lifetime of work. The average person with a bachelor's degree earns about $2.1 million over her lifetime. A person with a professional degree, such as an attorney or a doctor, typically earns about $4.4 million over a lifetime. Because the average person might begin work at age twenty and not retire until age sixty-five, a traditional employment period might encompass forty-five years.

By starting a home-based business and working hard for twenty years and investing your earnings, it's possible to greatly shorten your traditional employment and retire early, if that's your goal.

If you were to continue your home-based business for thirty years and it continued to give you an extra $20,000 to invest each year, you'd have over $3 million in thirty years.

Of course, you might spend some of that $20,000 annually. It's little fun to have extra income and not be able to purchase anything! The point of this discussion is to show you that a modest and non-growing home-based business can be an important tool in helping you retire early, achieve financial security, and even become a multimillionaire.

A home-based business whose earnings consistently grow can have a huge financial impact. For example, some businesses you could operate might earn $30,000 this year; $45,000 the next year; $60,000 the year after that; and $90,000 the year after that. You can see the powerful effect of having earnings that grow. Some businesses are better suited to growing earnings than others. One of the goals of this book is to help you focus upon your best opportunities—businesses that offer solid profitability and good potential for growth.

> Question: How do you anticipate growing earnings? What level of sales and earnings would you be happy with for your business?

Michael Dell founded Dell Computer in his college dorm room. He continued to grow the company aggressively. By 2003 at age 39, he was the eighteenth richest person in the United States with a net worth of $13 billion dollars.

Pierre Omidyar started eBay as a simple auction site to help his fiancée sell Pez dispensers from his living room in 1995. By age 36, he was worth $8.5 billion dollars and eBay became one of America's most popular brands.

Note: Guy Kawasaki author of *The Art of The Start: The Time-Tested, Battle-Hardened Guide for Anyone Starting Anything* claims the Pez dispenser story was only eBay PR and that Omidyar wanted to create a perfect marketplace. Anybody who operates an eBay business will tell you eBay is far from perfect! But, eBay has been a boon to many small sellers. Entire books, such as *Starting an eBay Business for Dummies* by Marsha Collier, have been written for eBay entrepreneurs.

Lillian Vernon was a housewife looking for extra income when she placed her first mail-order ad and invested $2,000 to start her new mail-order business. Within three months, the company was raking in tens of thousands of dollars in profitable orders. Today, Lillian Vernon Corporation has 20 million mail-order customers.

Clearly, Dell, Omidyar, and Vernon eventually had to move their business out of the house! And, along the way, they needed to encounter many topics and issues the average home-based business owner doesn't need to worry about, such as raising capital or managing employees. But many great entrepreneurial endeavors began as modest home-based businesses. And, as you've seen, even a modest non-growing or slow-growing home-based business can have a significant impact on your financial life.

What if, after several years of successfully running a home-based business, you become bored with your company or wish to pursue other endeavors? Rather than abandoning a profitable venture, you could begin thinking about how to modify the venture to better suit your changing interests. In this way, a home-based business can grow and change to accommodate your emerging interests. Unfortunately, small home businesses seldom have any market value. In other words, selling a home business is seldom a viable option.

But, first, we must decide upon the kind of business we want to start. This brings us to the importance of understanding the fundamental way in which we expect our company to earn money and change (or not) over the years.

Business Models

The first questions you must ask are:

> What kind of a business do I want to run?
> How will my business earn money?
> What are my goals for my business?
> What financial potential does my business idea have?
> Am I prepared to run this type of business?

Notice that I didn't include these questions:

> How much money will it take to start my business?
> What tools and equipment do I need to get started?

You could start many types of businesses based upon many different ideas, interests, or opportunities. But just because you're capable of doing something doesn't mean you should. You want to choose a good business opportunity that is right for you. After a bit of planning, you might find something you could do easily isn't the best opportunity for you. Or you might find something that's a great financial opportunity just doesn't let you do the things you want to do on a day-to-day basis or, in some other way, just isn't for you.

For example, many people want to run businesses based upon crafts and there's nothing wrong with that. Maybe you enjoy making wooden furniture. You think about making furniture and offering it for sale over the Internet. So, here is something you know how to do and something you like to do. Let's also assume your goal is to be able to earn at least $60,000 per year while working full-time at your endeavor. You also wish keep your business in your house and without employees.

The question becomes: Can this business endeavor allow me to achieve the goal of $60,000 in annual earnings? The answer is that you'll need to do some research. Offhand, we just don't know yet. Researching your endeavor's potential and making some very simple estimates are the first steps in business planning.

Many people jump head first into an endeavor without any planning only to discover later that their business can't meet their dreams or their goals. Then, after committing a year or two years of effort to the idea, they realize they need to change direction. Business planning will help you hone in on ideas that represent better opportunities. It will help prevent you from wasting time.

Let's suppose we make some basic assumptions. Suppose you estimate that each piece of furniture you sell can earn you $200 per unit in profit. Two of the first questions a new entrepreneur should ask are: 1) How many of the product in question do I think I can sell each year? and 2) How much profit per unit do I think I can make?

If you've already started asking yourself these questions, you're already thinking like an entrepreneur. How much money your endeavor can earn comes down to simple multiplication.

Multiply the number of products you think you can sell times the amount of money you think you can earn per sale:

Annual Profits = (Number of Products I Can Sell Per Year) (Profit Per Product Sold)

The above is a very basic formula. I hope you'll apply this formula to all of your ventures. It also applies to services. Ask how much of your service you'll be able to sell. While the formula is simple, a lot of research can go into estimating both the number of likely sales and the estimated profit per sale. Researching and estimating the numbers to plug into the formula will shed light on your proposed endeavor.

Let's begin with profit per product sold. The $200 estimate might have been made as follows: We estimated the sales price of one of our pieces of furniture. Then, we subtracted our estimated cost to build the piece to arrive at the net profit per unit.

Profit Per Unit Product = Sales Price of Product - Cost to Produce Product

Our first stab at the calculation was probably just a rough guess. Then, we might do some research to see what prices comparable pieces of furniture sell for and to more accurately calculate the cost to produce the piece. We need to confirm that our original estimates are valid. Or we need to learn if our initial estimates weren't accurate.

With $200 per unit as the estimated profit per unit, we can then calculate that, to earn $60,000 per year, we need to sell 300 furniture items per year. Now, if we've only allowed for material cost to produce the pieces and we've assumed that we were going to build all of the furniture ourselves, we might instantly see a problem.

For example, maybe it takes three days to build a piece. Working five days a week for fifty weeks a year only gives us

250 days to produce the 300 pieces. At most, we can only produce about 80 pieces. Thus, the profit potential of our business appears to be:

Annual Profit = ($200)(80) = $16,000.

That's rather low for full-time work! Notice how using the basic formula of trying to estimate your business's profit potential helps you distinguish profitable possibilities from less desirable ideas.

The natural thing people want to do is ask if they can raise their selling price, reduce their costs, or produce the item more efficiently.

Maybe, purchasing some special lathes and other machines could allow us to produce more furniture more quickly. If our profit estimates are correct, we need to finish about one piece per day. Is that realistic? Further, if you enjoy building furniture by hand, is this endeavor something you'd still like to do, if it becomes more automated or if it requires employees? If your production becomes more automated, will your furniture still be able to retain the same retail price and have the same quality you initially desired? How will your costs be affected by the costs of labor or of special automated equipment? And, can you still operate the business from your home if you change how it operates?

As you evaluate your endeavor you'll begin to see various constraints on what you're trying to do. Here it's the amount of time it takes you to produce one piece and, thus, the number of pieces you can produce in one year.

Now, if you can find a specialty niche that allows you to earn much more per unit, then you might be able to succeed at this endeavor. For example, if you can earn $1,000 per unit, selling 80 units a year allows you to make $80,000 per year, exceeding your targeted earnings. But, you might find you simply can't sell the item at the higher price. Or you can't sell enough of the item at the higher price to justify producing it.

This is often the disadvantage to labor-intensive crafts as a home-based business. You can earn money and you might enjoy it, but when all is said and done, you might find you can't earn enough money to make the venture truly desirable from a financial standpoint. When you consider the value of your time, the endeavor fails to be a good opportunity.

How much profit potential an endeavor must have to be considered desirable is something that's highly personal. For example, if you're looking to replace a full-time job paying $16,000 per year ($8 per hour), this online business might appeal to you.

Now, I know there's at least one guy out there who is either disappointed or miffed at me—because he wanted to sell furniture online, maybe through eBay. The numbers I used were only arbitrary, and it's possible a real venture in this direction could succeed. You need to estimate the numbers for yourself and come to your own conclusions about your proposed ideas. But, if the numbers say your idea should be abandoned, it's best abandoned. And, will people buy furniture online, given the shipping charges?

My purpose is to help you find a truly profitable home-based business opportunity. Just as importantly, the goal is to help you learn to evaluate potential opportunities realistically.

As a publisher who has helped other publishers and self-publishers start small publishing companies, I've sometimes bummed out an optimistic individual who wanted to self-publish a fictional book.

The truth as I see it is that self-publishing fiction is likely to lead to failure. For various reasons, the odds are stacked against the individual who tries this. And, I encourage new publishers to consider nonfiction books only. To those who really wish to be authors of fiction, I suggest that they might only want to self-publish initially with the intent of interesting a larger publisher in their work. And, unfortunately, that often fails also. The larger publisher has the resources to publish fiction successfully. But, don't expect self-published fiction to be profitable. This isn't only my view, but the view of many experienced book publishers.

Of course, there's always someone who breaks the mold and achieves something that others say probably won't work. The young author of *Eragon*, a fantasy novel, originally had the title successfully self-published by his father's publishing company. The novel went on to displace Harry Potter on the New York Times bestseller lists. But, by that time, the book had been sold to a larger publisher.

However, it's important for new entrepreneurs to understand what is known as the survivors' bias which makes many endeavors seem much more viable than they actually are. In many arenas, we tend to hear about the successful cases but don't see the failed ones.

For example, everyone has a success story of a young lady ambitiously moving to Hollywood at age 18 to become an actress. For example, Julia Roberts. But, we seldom hear the thousands of stories of young people who move to Hollywood, who have as much talent, who work just as hard, and who ultimately fail.

The lesson is never believe anecdotal evidence as an indicator of likely success. In particular, many companies specialize in trying to sell people various home-based business schemes. Very often these ventures don't benefit the majority of people who try them. I recommend you start your own home-based business without relying on any association to any company that claims it will help you become successful in your own home-based business. The information in books like this is all you need to get started. You're usually better off going it alone. If you make some initial effort to plan your venture, you'll more quickly find more profitable ventures to pursue.

Let's examine our basic equation again:

Annual Profits = (Number of Products I Can Sell Per Year)(Profit Per Product Sold)

Estimating the amount you make per sale is relatively easy. After subtracting production costs from a realistic selling price, we obtain an estimate of how much we might make per unit. This gives us an estimated profit per unit sold.

Estimating the number of products you can sell in a year is more difficult. In our woodworking case, we quickly found that something other than market demand limits us—our own productive capacity. This is true in general. *Either we are limited by how much we can produce or we are limited by how well our product will sell in the market.*

If we are limited by how much we can produce, that's a limit to our business model. This doesn't mean that our venture should be scrapped. It just means that we'll need to adjust how we do business to earn more money or we'll need to be satisfied with a lower level of profit, if we choose to remain with that venture.

I hope you see that, if your proposed venture involves producing crafts by hand from home, you'll have some inherent limit upon how much you'll be able to earn annually. This is true of many ventures. Somehow, the amount of money you can make is limited by your business model.

Consulting is often done from home. Consultants might charge $100 per hour for their time and find they can bill 1,500 hours per year. That puts a limit of about $150,000 upon their annual earnings. Again, the nature of the business they are trying to operate constrains their earnings.

Compare personal consulting to working as an intermediary who matches consultants with clients. Here there is no limit upon how much you can make annually. The business model is less constrained financially.

Using a fancy business term, we consider a business to be *extensible* if the business is easily capable of growing profits without changing the method the business uses to generate those profits. If the business must change its way of doing business to generate more profits, the business isn't extensible. A self-made craft business isn't easily extensible.

Question: Is your business idea extensible? Does this matter to you?

Exercise: Sit down with a pencil, paper, and your calculator. Estimate the profit potential of your proposed venture.

These rough estimates are sometimes called back-of-the-envelope calculations. Decide if you're happy with the rough estimate of your business idea's profit potential. If not, contemplate other business ideas or think about how you could modify your basic venture to make it more profitable.

Get in the habit of multiplying two numbers together—estimated sales and estimated profits per unit sold—for every business idea you have!

Distribution/Fulfillment Of Product Or Service

In addition to evaluating our capacity to produce our product or render our service, we must also consider the time and expense involved in the distribution and fulfillment of our product.

Who will ensure that our product gets to the customer and what cost is involved? Distribution capability determines how much of your product your company can sell.

For higher-priced products, distribution isn't usually as great an obstacle. For example, suppose you're a software designer who has written a computer program to help new entrepreneurs build online stores and to establish affiliate marketing programs. Affiliate marketing programs encourage other websites to link to your web page in exchange for a commission on any sales that are forwarded to you from the link. A small niche industry provides software to help people who want to create their own online affiliate marketing programs.

Affiliate Programs

The best-known affiliate program is that of the large company Amazon.com, and it's known as Amazon Associates. If you go to Amazon's web page and look for a link at the bottom of the page, it will describe their affiliate program. Studying Amazon's affiliate program will help you understand affiliate programs in general.

People who become Amazon Associates have websites, which they link to Amazon. Then, if a visitor follows the link to Amazon and purchases a book or other product, the Associate receives a commission for the sale. For example, for a $20 book purchased, the Associate might receive a 5% commission or $1.00. Both the Associate and Amazon benefit. The Associate gets the commission, and Amazon gets the sale and, possibly, a new long-term customer.

Because I enjoy reading and reviewing good business books, I created EntrepreneurBooks.com as an Amazon Associate. Each review of a book I post is linked to the book's page at Amazon.

Many other large companies have affiliate marketing programs of their own.

In addition to becoming an affiliate of another company and helping them sell their products for a commission, entrepreneurs can also use the power of affiliate marketing to sell their own products. Think of yourself as taking Amazon's role here. You pay a commission to others who help you generate sales.

Affiliate marketing is powerful, because it encourages other people to link to your site and to promote your products. If you go to google.com and search for "Affiliate Marketing" or "Starting An Affiliate Marketing Program," you'll find a wide range of resources to help you understand creating an affiliate marketing program of your own.

Suppose your program sells for $200 and you offer affiliates a $60 commission for each sale of your program they generate. (Here, we're talking about selling the program through your own affiliate network. Don't confuse an affiliate *marketing program* with the *computer program* which we're discussing *as the product*.) Assume your software costs $20 to produce. You earn $120 per program sold, and you sell it directly to individual customers from your own website. Most of your sales result from inbound links from other websites which are your affiliates.

If you sell 1,000 programs per year, you can earn $120,000. Packing and shipping 1,000 units per year only amounts to packing and shipping four per day, Monday through Friday. That's not a substantial investment of time, probably taking well under half an hour per day. Even if you sold 2,000 per year and were earning $240,000 per year, you might only need to spend an hour a day on fulfillment activities.

Now, let's consider the other extreme—a relatively low-priced product. Suppose you produce a booklet that makes you $5 profit each. To earn $50,000 per year, you'd need to pack and ship 10,000 booklets. That's about forty per day, Monday through Friday. Now, fulfillment time becomes significant. You might or might not want to do fulfillment yourself.

One option would be to hire a part-time worker to help with your packing and shipping. This would reduce your profits slightly and would allow you to concentrate your time into avenues that are more likely to grow your earnings or promote your products. However, having employees isn't ideal for a home-based business.

The purpose of zoning laws is to prevent substantial commercial activity from taking place in residential neighborhoods. Your neighbors might not want several of your employees parking in the street! In this way, having employees can endanger your home-based business by exposing it to zoning laws. Also, having employees work from your home poses other issues, such as what happens if an employee is injured? And, where will the employee work inside your home? Do you want employees wandering around in your house?

If you employ one of your children, that would negate many of the disadvantages to hiring employees. You could pay your child a reasonable wage for the work performed. You might find that you could hire one part-time employee and do so sufficiently discretely, so that zoning doesn't become an issue.

However, even if you're happy with the concept of one part-time employee, you need to understand that, at this point, you become an employer, subject to all the legal requirements of having employees. You'll need to withhold income tax from their wages, for example. And, you'll need to fill out employment tax forms, such as the W-2, 940, and 941. Failure to do so could result in penalties from the IRS. And, at a very basic level, management and supervisory skills become important. You'll need to train your employee and be sure that he performs his duties adequately.

Many home-based business owners who hire one part-time employee to do product fulfillment find that it would just be simpler to do the tasks themselves! I call this hitting the employee barrier. When you add in the time to administer payroll, provide training, and supervise an employee, you might find you could have done the work yourself in the same time! Once a company has three to five employees or more, I believe the employee barrier is much less of a problem. But, you don't want that many employees in a typical home-based business.

If you contemplate hiring one part-time employee, you might decide to make him or her a part-time administrative assistant, who can handle things such as phone screening, letter preparation, etc. That will often free up much of your time. Hiring a virtual assistant is another option. Virtual assistants are secretaries who work from home. Another option is to hire someone to help with non-business household duties, such as mowing the lawn or cleaning.

Once you have employees, employee turnover becomes important. One great employee who stays with you a long time can be a godsend. But, if you find you must constantly train someone new to the job, having an employee will probably be more stress than it's worth.

For most home-based businesses, I'd recommend against having employees, especially for product fulfillment duties. Fortunately, you have another option which will allow you to fulfill a large number of orders. You can outsource product fulfillment. There are companies that specialize in providing picking, packaging, and mailing of orders. You'll find this service reduces your profit per unit. But, if you must sell a large number of items, a fulfillment company might be a good option.

Outsourcing of fulfillment and distribution is a common practice in the publishing industry. Most book publishers sell the majority of their titles through book distributors and book wholesalers. And, many smaller publishers don't store or ship books. They use fulfillment companies to do the shipping.

Home-based business owners need to give special thought to product distribution and fulfillment, because they may lack the resources to fill orders themselves. The costs of distribution must be considered when evaluating the profit potential of a business.

For example, in book publishing, it's common for an exclusive distributor to receive 60% of the cover price of the book. This means, for a $20 book, the book distributor receives $12.00 and the publisher receives $8.00. Part of the $12.00 discount is passed on to book retailers.

While that sounds like giving up a lot of potential profit to the distributor, consider that printed books are shipped directly to the distributor and the publisher never needs to handle the books. The distributor sells the books and handles all fulfillment functions. For a smaller publisher selling 20,000 books per year, the fulfillment job would easily become a burden.

When evaluating the profitability of a product with a back-of-the-envelope calculation, be sure you're using the price you actually receive for your product. The amount you receive must allow for whatever percentage goes to wholesalers, distributors, and retailers. For example, if you use a distributor, you won't receive the full retail price of your product, but only a portion of it. Consider the formula:

Profit Per Product Unit = Sales Price Of Product - Cost To Produce Product

If we sell through a distributor, we need to use the net amount we receive from the distributor as the "Sales Price of Product" and not some arbitrarily suggested retail price.

> Exercise: Consider the $20 book discussed previously which is sold through a distributor at a 60% discount. Assume each book costs $2.00 to produce and marketing expenses are $1.00 per book. Assume no other expenses. Calculate the profit potential of selling 30,000 books per year (Answer: $150,000).

With a distribution mechanism in place, the small book publisher is not limited by how many books he can pack and ship. The publisher could sell 20,000 books, 50,000 books, or 100,000 books per year and operate the company from her home.

In addition to companies specializing in fulfillment, wholesaling, or distribution, home-based entrepreneurs can also partner with larger companies to gain the distribution power of the larger company.

Consider the toy industry. Suppose you've invented a new board game and you wish to sell it in retail stores. Trying to distribute the game to retail stores yourself would prove difficult, because stores don't want to deal with many small vendors. Plus, you'd need to have another company manufacture your game.

However, if a larger game company becomes interested in your game, it might pay you a royalty for each game sold. The larger company would take care of all manufacturing and sales distribution. This essentially gives you unlimited sales potential.

When Chris Haney and Scott Abbott sat around playing Scrabble one day in 1979, they decided they should invent their own board game. After a bit of thinking, they came up with the idea of a game where people would answer questions and move a piece around the board with each correct answer. Tokens would be collected when landing on key board locations and answering correctly. The game was Trivial Pursuit.

Haney and Abbott partnered with the established game company, Selchow and Righter, which promoted Trivial Pursuit at the New York Toy Fair. The game became a smash hit, and, by 1984, over 20 million copies had been sold. By 2004, gross sales of Trivial Pursuit would top one billion dollars.

If your product is protected by intellectual property law, such as copyright or patent law, licensing rights to a larger company may offer significant profit potential with little or no work on the distribution side.

> Question: Is your product capable of being protected by a patent or a copyright? If so, do you think partnering with a larger, established company would be beneficial? What are the estimated costs to distribute your product as a percentage of the retail selling price? How do you anticipate handling product delivery or fulfillment? Must the way you distribute your product change as your company grows?
>
> Question: Do you anticipate needing to hire employees for your home-based business? If so, do you still feel this venture is suited to being operated from home? Do you plan to grow the venture beyond your home?

Marketing And Sales

Now that we've tried to estimate the profit potential of our idea and we've contemplated distribution methods, we need to turn our attention to the marketing and sales of our product or service. At a fundamental level, we need to ask: Who will buy our product? And, how will we make these people aware of our product?

It's crucial to point out that we will seldom know how well our product will be received in the marketplace. Consider the book series based upon the Harry Potter character. No one could have predicted that the book would go on to sell over 250 million copies and make its author a billionaire. Conversely, many products that seem viable fail in the marketplace.

The only real way to test a product's marketability is to create the product and see if it sells. Depending upon your product or service, your marketing will take different approaches.

For example, for marketing the affiliate marketing software discussed previously, nearly all the marketing would be done online. A website would be created to sell the product. Then, awareness of the site would be generated and inbound links created to the site.

However, suppose you're operating an electrical contracting or a roofing company from your home. These businesses typically require employees, but that isn't much of an issue, because all work is done away from your home. Marketing this type of business would probably involve getting an ad in the local Yellow Pages. As you grow, you might also consider radio or TV advertising.

The type of business you contemplate determines your approach to sales and marketing. What works for one type of business won't necessarily work for another. For example, for the roofing company, a strong online presence wouldn't be particularly valuable. For the affiliate software seller, an ad in the Yellow Pages probably wouldn't be useful.

Consider the following marketing avenues and ask which might be useful to your business:

Creating An Online Website
Direct Mail Marketing
Telemarketing
Creating A Catalog To Give To Potential Customers
Yellow Pages Advertising
Creating Yard Signs
Handing Out Business Cards
Attending Conventions To Market Your Product
Trying To Generate Word of Mouth Referrals
Radio Or TV Advertising
Generating Free Publicity
Advertising In Magazines Or Newspapers

Now that you've contemplated how marketing relates to your particular product, draw up a marketing plan for your product. Your marketing plan should focus on one to three of the best ways you believe you can generate sales of your product or service.

Using the roofing company as an example, we might focus upon the following:

Yellow Pages Advertising
Creating Yard Signs To Post Where A Job Is Being Done
Having Business Cards
Asking For Referrals

The new roofing entrepreneur is likely to wonder just how effective those marketing avenues will be. One of the best ways to find effective marketing methods for a particular business is to examine competing businesses and see how they market their products or services. This is sometimes called competitive intelligence or just doing industry research.

As you create a business model, it pays to study your company's industry and try to learn about similar businesses.

Now that we've evaluated the potential profitability of our endeavor, considered distribution and fulfillment, and, finally, marketing, we have a good sense of how our business will earn money. This will be the foundation of your business model. It will be your plan of business. While you don't need to write a formal business plan, it's good to plan ahead. Your plans will probably change as you gain experience in your industry. This experience will help you refine your business model and make it more effective.

Missing Skills, Accreditation, and Industry Experience

Next, we consider if we're prepared to run the type of business we anticipate. For example, if we knew absolutely nothing about the roofing business, we'd be hard pressed to begin operations.

Similarly, if you wished to become a financial planner, but had no experience or certifications, such as a CFP, it might be more difficult to get started. Work on building these skills, accreditations, and industry experience. Draw up a list of industry specific skills and credentials that would be useful to you. Evaluate how much time and effort would be required to attain them. Study your industry!

In my book *Thinking Like An Entrepreneur*, I have a chapter entitled *Men Are Cheaper Than Guns* in which I argue that one of the best ways to get skills is to hire others with the skills (You can read this chapter online at ThinkingLike.com). Many people feel that they must do everything themselves. But, sometimes, certain jobs can be outsourced.

For example, the founder of Intuit, the maker of the popular financial planning software Quicken, had the basic idea for how the personal finance program would work. But, he wasn't a professional programmer with the skills to actually write the computer program. He hired a computer programmer to help him create the software program Quicken. That allowed him to get a program to market quickly without learning computer programming.

For a home-based entrepreneur, hiring full-time employees usually isn't desirable, because often the home-based businessperson wishes to remain a company of one and doesn't want to deal with the hassles of having employees. However, certain jobs can be outsourced to independent contractors.

What if you don't have the cash to pay a professional whose talents you could use? One possibility would be to consider entering a partnership. For example, rather than paying cash to get a computer programmer to develop some software idea you have, you could offer a percentage of any profits the software makes or offer to pay a flat royalty for each product sold.

This type of licensing reduces the amount of cash you need to develop products, but often leads to paying more for product development in the long run. For example, something that might have cost you $10,000 to create if you paid cash might eventually cost you $500,000 in royalties instead. However, your downside risk is reduced if the product doesn't have market demand.

When you reduce your financial risk when starting a venture or launching a new product, it's called risk shifting. Risk shifting involves finding ways to reduce your risk so that a product failure won't financially harm you greatly.

General Business Learning Versus Industry-Specific Learning

It's important to note that there are two spheres of knowledge you'll need to successfully create your business. The first is a general understanding of business.

For example, you might need to understand topics such as selecting insurance for your home-based business or learning a bit about how basic accounting and bookkeeping work. This information is available from many sources, such as this book. Although this knowledge might seem overwhelming at first, it's actually quite easy to learn, because you have a wide range of resources to help you. And, once it's learned, it's learned. You'll be using the same knowledge over and over again. And, this information is largely independent of the type of business you start, be it a garage-door repair firm or a biotech company.

Once you've filled out one IRS 1099 form to employ an independent contractor, you've essentially learned how to fill out the form. Once you've paid your business taxes with Schedule C, doing it again the next year will be easier. Once you've learned how to use a basic accounting program, entering data will be easy for you.

The second sphere of knowledge is industry specific knowledge. For example, if you're a game inventor, you'll need to learn about toy fairs and how best to market your product to get good distribution. You'll also need to understand product licensing, typical royalties paid for games, etc. For many businesses, including the game industry, an understanding of negotiation and contracts is useful.

This second sphere of knowledge is usually more inaccessible. I believe that many new business owners neglect this sphere. And, I believe that's one reason many new entrepreneurs fail. *Learning about your specific industry is probably the most important thing you can do when starting a new business.*

How Should You Learn About Your Industry?

First, do a google search of some basic terms related to your industry. For example, if you're a game developer, search for phrases like "game licensing" and "board game distribution."

As you learn more about your industry, search for new terms you learn that relate to your business.

Your online search will probably turn up many informative websites. Today, you'll also find many quality e-mail discussion lists where specific industries and businesses are discussed. For example, there are several high-quality e-mail discussion lists that serve the small press community. Some of these discussion groups are quite specialized, such as focusing upon computer book publishing, fantasy book publishing, or print-on-demand publishing. This is a chance to get advice from some very knowledgeable and experienced people in your industry.

Second, see what trade associations serve your industry. Many industries have professional associations that can help you learn more about an industry. See what conventions they offer. This might be an opportunity to network with those in a business similar to yours. Meeting others who operate similar businesses can provide valuable insight.

Third, check amazon.com or your favorite bookstore for books that discuss the industry or starting a business in the industry. For example, for new publishers, there is a wide range of quality books about starting a publishing company, including *The Self Publishing Manual* by Dan Poynter and my own book, *How To Start And Run A Small Book Publishing Company*. Because many publishers are also writers, you'll have many quality resources for learning to self-publish a book.

However, if you're interested in starting a financial consulting firm, there are far fewer resources. Many financial consultants write books, but about personal finance, not about starting a financial planning firm.

Before posting questions to any industry e-mail discussion lists you find, be sure to read about your industry first. If you post very basic questions that are covered in the widely-available literature about your industry, some possible mentors will not respond, because they'll feel you haven't put enough effort into researching the business. If you ask more complex, specific questions, you'll usually get better answers.

Also, you might find some print magazines that serve your industry.

Some areas, such as real estate development, have many quality books, but they also have many books by get-rich-quick gurus selling dubious advice. As a new entrepreneur, it's important to learn to separate the good advice from the bad. For real estate, one website evaluating various gurus is JohnTReed.com.

Usually, anything promoted as a "work at home opportunity" or as a "business opportunity" isn't. For example, late night infomercials will tell you that, if you purchase a company's information, they'll set you up running your own profitable Internet business and they'll supply all the products. You should usually pass on such offers. If it were trivially easy to build a website and sell many of those products at high profit, the company would just do this themselves!

Possibly, if you have a sales orientation, you might consider acting as a sales agent for another company's products. But, again, approach any claims of likely profits with skepticism. If you conceive of the idea yourself for your business and follow a path completely of your own choosing, you'll probably be more successful in the long run.

Network Marketing And MLM

One of the areas many new home-based business people fall into are network marketing or MLM (multi-level marketing). Approach any such "opportunities" with caution. Many of these "opportunities" are nothing more than a scam.

Before joining any network marketing organization, do a google.com search of the organization. You'll often find sites that share the experiences of others who tried the MLM. Typically, these organizations will claim you can earn huge profits by joining their organization. Often, the typical earnings of members is trivial. Be skeptical of any glowing endorsements of various network marketing plans. Some of these companies resort to placing false endorsements.

That said, there are legitimate network marketing opportunities. Usually, these companies are looking for salespeople for their products. If you like the product and have good sales skills, you might find you can do well with the product. Just be sure you research the product adequately. And, be sure you're OK with the concept of selling to people you already know, because that's usually one of the objectives of network marketing.

Tupperware comes to mind as one of the first products successfully marketed via network marketing. Mary Kay Cosmetics is another well-established product that has many legitimate sellers.

There is an interesting video about the history of Tupperware called *American Experience - Tupperware*. Another book which describes the history of Tupperware is *Tupperware: The Promise of Plastic in 1950s America* by Alison Clarke. For people interested in understanding the history of network marketing, I recommend these resources.

Tupperware was invented by Earl Tupper in the 1940s. Incidentally, Tupper also patented a fish-powered boat, with a picture of a huge fish strapped to the bottom of a boat! However, the crucial aspect of Tupperware's success was the Tupperware party and network marketing as created by Brownie Wise, a single mom who worked to promote Tupperware. She focused upon selling and creating a sales-based force.

Exercise And Question: In the chapter *Do You Want To Start A Home-Based Business?* I discuss the book by John Miner and the four personality types he attributes to successful entrepreneurs. Watch the video or DVD *American Experience - Tupperware* (try getting it through your local library using interlibrary loan, or it's available from amazon.com) and

> classify the personality types of Earl Tupper and Brownie Wise. Do you think Earl Tupper could have succeeded without Brownie Wise?
>
> Question: Compare network marketing to Internet affiliate marketing. How are the two methods similar? How are they different?

If you create a product that could benefit from network marketing, consider using commissioned salespeople to sell your product. The huge success of Tupperware, for example, is largely due to the company's ability to attract homemakers to sell the product. Granted, the plastic bowls and containers worked well, and this was also a contributing factor to their success.

> Question: Do you need a personal sales force for your product? How will the sales force be paid? Would network marketing be a viable option for selling your product? Do you like the concept of network marketing, or do you find it unappealing?

While some people like network marketing, others view it as little better than a pyramid scam that companies try to get people to pawn off on their friends. Each entrepreneur must make his or her own call about the legitimacy of using network marketing techniques to sell products.

Franchising is another area where care is required before jumping. There are other books that discuss purchasing and evaluating a franchise in detail. I'd search on amazon.com to find some books about evaluating franchises, if buying a franchise is your plan. The Federal Trade Commission also publishes a booklet called *A Consumer Guide to Buying a Franchise* (www.ftc.gov).

Personally, I'm not a big fan of a home-based business owner buying into a franchise. Many home businesses that can be purchased as franchise opportunities can also be set up as fully private businesses for less cost and offer more upside financial potential.

Don't forget that the reverse also applies. Possibly, you need sales agents for your own products or services. Will some form of franchising or network marketing work for you?

If you franchise operations to others, you'll need to learn about the regulations that affect franchises so you don't run afoul of the law. Because of the huge potential for fraudulent franchise offers, franchising is regulated.

Cookie Cutter Business Models

Many popular business books emphasize trying to develop what amounts to a cookie-cutter business model or a "turn-key business." You set the business model up, and it makes endless profits for you with little ongoing work from you. You put the key in, turn it, and the business generates profits for you. *The E-Myth Revisited: Why Most Small Businesses Don't Work and What to Do About It* by Michael Gerber is one book looking at this concept.

Most businesses, however, require considerable and consistent involvement from the owner. Successful serial entrepreneurs, knowledgeable angel investors, and most experienced business people will tell you that the business model or business plan is secondary to the entrepreneurship team.

The best business plans often change several times before success is realized, and this process involves considerable feedback from the target market. The business plan meets reality, and reality changes the plan. The people running the business make success happen. Not the idea. Not the business model. Although a bad business model can do you in.

Thus, while books, such as *The E-Myth Revisited: Why Most Small Businesses Don't Work and What to Do About It*, can be loaded with good ideas to help you think about how to operate your business more efficiently, never expect a business to be truly "turn key." Consider it more like driving a car. You must turn the key to get the motor started, but if you don't pay attention after you get going, you'll crash into something and hurt yourself.

Your business might outsource a tremendous amount of work. But, you'll still need to manage your business operations. No business model will relieve you of that responsibility.

Chapter 2
Do You Want To Start A Home-Based Business?

Given that you're reading this book, the answer is probably "yes."

Some of the reasons people start home-based businesses include:

- A Desire To Spend More Time With Family Or Eliminate Day Care Hassles
- To Earn More Money
- To Earn Extra Part-Time Income
- To Be Your Own Boss
- To Avoid Daily Commutes And Save Time

Saving time is a major reason many people like the idea of starting a home-based business. Over a twenty-year period a person commuting two hours a day (one hour each way) spends the equivalent of five working years driving. Essentially, you're working twenty-five years for twenty years of pay.

If you work *at home*, you'll be able to avoid this daily commute. However, if you must travel for your home-based business, you won't save any commuting time. For example, if you're a home-based house inspector, you'll need to travel to the homes you inspect.

With day care costs rising, many moms and dads wish to spend more time at home, but find they need two incomes to support their families. A home-based business might offer a good way for a parent to earn extra money while remaining at home during the day.

There are also downsides to operating a home-based business. Downsides typically include:

- Difficulty Separating Your Work Life From Your Personal Life
- Less Certain Income
- Potentially, A Feeling Of Isolation

Curious cases often involve parents who wish to spend more time at home with their kids and save money on day care. They start home-based businesses and later decide to enroll their children in day care so they have time to work on their home-based business. Sometimes, the idea of the home business is good, but the demands of watching the children makes getting work done impossible. So, the routine becomes getting up in the morning, taking the kids to day care, coming home to work, and picking the kids up at the end of the day!

After you start your business, you'll learn if your plans will work. Can you manage your business goals with home responsibilities? Or, will you need to make adjustments in your home life?

For example, do you have a quiet place to work? If not, you might need to modify your home slightly to create a better work environment.

Time management is crucial for a home-based business owner. You'll need to balance the time you work with the time you do home duties and the time you play. Typically, you'll completely set your own hours and schedule. This can be a boon for some, but it can be the kiss of death for others.

Home-based entrepreneurs need to learn effective time management. In particular, a home-based entrepreneur could start the day off with a walk, go play some golf, come home and read a book, watch some news on TV, and before he knows it, the work day is over and nothing related to business has been achieved!

For one day, that's probably okay. Flexibility to take it easy when you want is one of the advantages of working for yourself from home. However, if you procrastinate day-after-day and do little for your business, your company probably won't be very successful. *I believe one of the primary reasons some home-based businesses fail is because it's too easy to divert time away from the business.*

Deciding What You Really Want To Do With Your Life

It's possible you haven't decided exactly what kind of home-based business you want to start. Some books, such as *Best Home Businesses for the 21ˢᵗ Century* by Paul and Sarah Edwards, list several profiles of different home-based businesses you could start, if you're seeking specific business types to examine.

I'm a big fan of reading about various entrepreneurs and the businesses they operate as a guide to help you develop your entrepreneurial skills and gain insight to help you operate your own business. Read features about local entrepreneurs in the business section of your local newspaper. Clip and save especially interesting articles you think may help you in the future, either because the articles give you inspiration or insight or just because they describe an especially unique business you never knew existed.

Consider subscribing to small business magazines, such as *Inc. Magazine* (inc.com) or *Entrepreneur Magazine* (entrepreneur.com). Reading books that feature or profile several different entrepreneurs is a good idea. One book I especially like is *What No One Ever Tells You About Starting Your Own Business: Real Life Start-Up Advice from 101 Successful Entrepreneurs* by Jan Norman.

Many successful entrepreneurs stumble into their businesses, usually because the entrepreneur has previous industry experience. That experience gives the entrepreneur insight into the industry and helps her see opportunities that industry outsiders don't see (it also helps entrepreneurs build personal connections). If you contemplate operating a certain kind of business, consider applying for a job with a similar company to help you learn about the industry. Only stay at the job two years or so. Consider it on-the-job learning.

While studying existing businesses and business ideas proposed by others is one way to find a business to run, another approach is contemplating what skills you personally enjoy using and seeking a business that matches those skills.

Several career books are useful if you take this approach:

• *I Don't Know What I Want, but I Know It's Not This: A Step-By-Step Guide to Finding Gratifying Work* by Julie Jansen
• *What Color Is Your Parachute?* by Richard Nelson Bolles
• *Now, Discover Your Strengths: The Revolutionary program that shows you how to develop your unique talents and strengths—and those of the people you manage* by Marcus Buckingham and Donald O. Clifton, Ph.D.

For example, consider becoming a literary agent. Several questions might come to mind. What exactly does a literary agent do, anyway? What skills are involved? Would I enjoy using those skills? Is this a business that personally suits me? How can I begin learning about the business? What would I need to do to get started?

While having a personal connection to an established literary agency might help you get an internship, you might find you need to initially learn about the business through books and articles. Ask: Is there somebody I could interview about being a literary agent? Does anybody I know have a contact with a literary agent?

Searching amazon.com, we find several books about the industry, including: *The Agent: Personalities, Politics, & Publishing* by Arthur M. Klebanoff.

By reading this book, we gain some insights into what is involved in being a literary agent. Even if we hadn't known it before, we learn that being a successful agent is highly dependent upon networking and building personal connections to publishers, acquisition editors, magazine editors, and others who are poised to promote a book. Being on the telephone a lot and interacting with many people is a natural part of the job. Negotiation skills are valuable, as is a very basic understanding of typical book publishing contracts. It's probably best, but not essential, to be located in New York. If you wish to be a film script agent, California is the place to be.

This information helps us decide if being a literary agent is a viable path for us. For example: Do we enjoy networking? Is it something we do naturally? Do we have or will we be able to build the connections required?

By matching the strengths, skills, and personality traits usually required to be successful in a particular type of business (or career path) with our inherent talents, strengths, and skills, we can see if the business is a good fit for us. To do this, we must have an understanding of what we enjoy doing the most (personal insight into our talents and dislikes). We must also have an understanding of what's required to be successful along a particular career or entrepreneurship path (information about what's actually done in this type of business). Lacking either of these, it's possible to start a business that we won't enjoy and one that won't bring us happiness. Without happiness and personal fulfillment, success is also less likely.

Stepping Stone Opportunities

Once you've begun pursuing business opportunities that appeal to you, you'll acquire new information and knowledge that will often lead you in different directions and open up new business opportunities for you. It's precisely this information that gives people with industry experience an advantage.

Consider ex-British paratrooper Mark Burnett who ran an athletic competition called Eco-Challenge. To offer a decent financial return to his event's sponsors, Burnett realized that he should try to get TV exposure for the event. This led him to produce some basic TV coverage of Eco-Challenge. (These competitions were held throughout the world. Consider it a home business for somebody who didn't like staying at home!)

In 1996, Burnett received an Emmy Award for his TV production of Eco-Challenge. People enjoyed watching real people compete in events. Having learned about TV production, Burnett went on to produce the TV show *Survivor* which is a mix of competition and social drama.

People enjoyed the social drama of real life. Burnett then produced the reality show *The Apprentice*, which is hosted by real estate mogul Donald Trump and which became the number one rated TV show in 2003.

Today, Burnett's popular reality-based TV shows earn him licensing royalties of about $2 million per episode. He's earned a slew of Emmy Awards and was named one of the 101 most powerful people in entertainment by *Entertainment Weekly*.

In fact, Burnett is known as "The Poster Boy For Reality TV" and has changed TV programming forever by introducing and developing the reality-based TV show. (Burnett is also author of the book *Dare to Succeed: How to Survive and Thrive in the Game of Life*, and I believe he has a new book coming out. He came to America with no money, and unable to find a chauffeur job, he became a nanny, before succeeding as a TV producer. Because of his paratrooper-nanny background, he's also been labeled "commando nanny.")

The point isn't that you should try to produce your own reality-based TV show. Today, reality TV shows are sprouting up like weeds! But, do examine the cycle of how following a business opportunity leads to new challenges, insights, and opportunities:

1) Following a business opportunity, hobby, or desire can lead to experience and new insights. You wouldn't necessarily expect that producing an athletic competition would lead to learning about TV production and eventually lead to becoming a TV producer. Many entrepreneurs might have just said: "I don't know anything about producing content for TV, so I can't follow up on this." Sometimes, you need to be willing to step outside of your comfort zone. That's where your learning will occur and sometimes where you'll find your best opportunities.

2) Seeing an opportunity or need *related or somehow connected* to what you're currently doing and learning more about it. Eco-Challenge was initially the product and TV a way of helping to promote it. But, Burnett saw that producing reality TV programming was a good opportunity for him, totally independent of Eco-Challenge. As he did more, he learned more.

3) Learning about the new opportunity and experimenting with variations. *Survivor* was essentially a spin-off of Burnett's original competition, having a physical component. But, as we saw, viewers are also interested in social drama, which is one of the elements of the business-focused hit *The Apprentice.*

A good question: Why didn't the established TV producers see the potential value of reality-based TV programming? Sometimes a fresh perspective from outside a field pays off.

The above cycle of trying something out, learning more as you do it, and then moving in new and more profitable directions based upon what you learn might seem obvious to individual, personal development.

Surprisingly, big companies go through a similar learning cycle. *The Entrepreneurial Mindset: Strategies for Continuously Creating Opportunity in an Age of Uncertainty* by Rita Gunther McGrath and Ian MacMillan describes how companies create "Stepping-Stone Options" which help them gain entry into new endeavors. Small forays are made to gain information upon which future success is built.

Personal Success Characteristics

Some new entrepreneurs might wonder if they have what it takes to be successful running their own business. I tend to feel that if you choose a field you love, have persistence, and are willing to work hard, your chances of success are good.

Professors of entrepreneurship have studied personal characteristics associated with success in business in more detail. John Miner, author of *The Four Routes To Entrepreneurial Success*, studied 100 New York entrepreneurs and determined that successful entrepreneurs tended to have one of four basic personality types. He classified these entrepreneurs as either:

• Personal Achievers. These people had a strong motivation to be successful. They were achievement-oriented.

• Super Sales People. These people have a natural ability to sell. Some of the most successful business people are primarily good at generating sales. They tend to be people-oriented.

• Skilled Managers. These people tend to manage employees well.

• Great Idea Generators. These people tend to be product-focused and innovative.

As the founder of a home-based business, you probably don't have many employees, so being a skilled people manager probably won't help you much. If you have substantial management experience and skill, you might want to consider growing your company as rapidly as possible to a size where it outgrows your home, has several employees, and allows you to bring your management skills into action. Or, you might want to consider a home-based business that hires employees who work at job locations away from your home, such as being a construction contractor. Don't choose a *home-based* business if it limits the use of your natural talents.

Conversely, a home-based business is a natural choice for an entrepreneur who isn't a natural manager and who doesn't want to manage employees. As a one-person business, all you need to manage is yourself!

Great salespeople have a big advantage in most businesses, but many successful home-based business owners aren't self-promotional. They aren't natural salespeople. If you lack sales skills or you don't want to do personal selling, be sure to avoid a business that requires personal selling. For example, you could easily operate an Internet-based company, but acting as a literary agent wouldn't be a natural fit.

Many home-based business owners tend to be personal achievers or idea people. They want to do well and tend to take care of details. They like to set goals and achieve them. They like to come up with ideas and find ways to make their ideas profitable.

Never let anyone tell you that you must have certain characteristics to be successful in every type of business. *Find businesses that match your natural talents and what you want to do.* Select your home business from among the businesses that cater to your natural strengths. That will probably give you the highest level of satisfaction and success.

Overcoming The Fear Of Starting A Business

> "There is one elementary truth, the ignorance of which kills countless ideas and splendid plans. The moment one definitely commits oneself, then Providence moves too. All sorts of things occur to help one that would never otherwise have occurred...Whatever you can do or dream you can, begin it. Boldness has genius, power, and magic to it. Begin it now." —Goethe.

What if you're afraid to start a home business? Some new entrepreneurs read about starting a business. Then, they look into doing it and never take action. Sometimes, they just seem overwhelmed by the process of getting started.

Fear is a natural protector. It keeps us from doing stupid things (usually!). But, we're often frightened of the unknown, even if venturing into the unknown could have a great positive impact on our lives. Consider Mark Burnett who we mentioned previously. If he hadn't been willing to try new things and move in new directions, rather than being one of the 101 most powerful people in entertainment, he might still be a nanny!

To help you overcome the fear of getting started, consider reducing your risk as you start your new venture. Begin part-time. Don't take on large overhead expenses. Then, contemplate just how much you really are risking to get started. Make a short list of what you're really risking. Usually, you'll discover the actual risk is very small. And, even if you fail, you can at least say you tried. That's more than many people do.

We sometimes say "I can't" or "I don't know how" and then decide not to act. It's fine to say "I don't want to" and decide not to pursue a course of action. But if you feel you really want to start a home business and you have a basically good idea, I think the best way to overcome any fears is to get started.

Jump to the state resource section at the end of this book, find your state, and answer the business research questions there. Choose and register a business name for your new company. Apply for any local licenses your business requires. Then, jump to the section *Fifteen Steps In Starting A Home-Based Business* and begin working on those items that remain. You're now on the path to owning your own home business!

Chapter 3
Naming Your Business

Essentially all a sole proprietor needs to do to get started in business is choose a business name, file for a certificate of assumed name, and apply for any necessary state and local business licenses the business might require. Sole proprietors without employees usually don't need to file any special forms with the federal government or the IRS to register their businesses.

Whenever you operate a business under any name other than your own full legal name, you're usually expected to file a certificate of assumed name, also known as a DBA (Doing Business As).

Certificates of assumed names are managed by your state government, so check with them to get the full filing requirements and find out about any fees. Often, filing a certificate of assumed name amounts to nothing more than filling out a one-page form and sending in a small fee. See the state resources section at the back of this book for more information about assumed names in your state.

Some states require publication of the assumed name in a qualified newspaper. This means you must take out a small ad saying you're doing business under that name. The purpose of such ads is to inform the local community of the true owner behind a business. This requirement is somewhat archaic, given the large number of small businesses which do business via mail order and the internet and which have few, if any, local customers.

In any case, it's important to follow your state's instructions fully when filing the certificate of assumed name. If publication in a qualified newspaper is required and you fail to do so, that could cause you difficulty down the road, because the name hasn't been properly and completely registered. Publication in the newspaper is considered part of the filing. Be sure to keep a copy of the newspaper notification.

When filing your name, your state will check to be sure your desired name is sufficiently distinct from other local business names. For example, if you want to name your company "Tony's Tennis Stringing" and another company already uses the name "Tony's Tennis Racket Stringing," you'll probably need to select another name, because your state will want to be sure consumers can distinguish between the two competing companies.

Contact your secretary of state for more information about name searches (see the state resource section). Most secretaries of state also allow you to file for state trademark use of the name to prevent other companies in the state from using your company name.

Because it's possible your first name choice will be denied, it's a good idea to have a couple of alternative company names. However, just because your name is accepted on a state-wide level doesn't guarantee you have the full legal right to use the name. Possibly, a federal trademark registration will prevent you from using the name. See the chapter about Intellectual Capital for more information about trademarks.

It's even possible for you to file for a trademark of your business name at both the state and federal level, have the trademark accepted, and still wind up in a lawsuit over a name.

This happened, for example, to entrepreneur Scott Smith who started a public relations firm for entrepreneurs and named his company EntrepreneurPR. He trademarked the name EntrepreneurPR successfully, but was sued by Entrepreneur Media, Inc., the publisher of *Entrepreneur Magazine*, which holds trademarks of the word "entrepreneur."

Due to the time and cost of legal battles, most smaller businesses will want to avoid naming conflicts.

Choosing An Effective Small Business Name

When naming your company, keep these points in mind:

• Choose a name that is memorable. If people can't remember your company name, it makes finding your company or getting word-of-mouth referrals more difficult. Avoid names that are difficult to spell or pronounce. Avoid excessively long names.

• Consider choosing a name *somewhat* descriptive or suggestive of what you do. Descriptive names make your product or service clear to customers, who will immediately understand what your company does. But, names that are too descriptive might be difficult to remember and might sound dull. Further, you'll have more difficulty protecting an identity through trademarks if you choose a descriptive name.

• Choose a name that allows for sufficient business growth. For example, "Tony's Tennis Stringing" makes it clear that Tony restrings tennis rackets, but if Tony starts to provide tennis lessons, his name doesn't reflect this. If he planned only to string rackets, the name might be okay.

• Avoid names that give inappropriate connotations or associations. For example, "Brown Fruit Company" isn't a good name, because "Brown" might be considered to modify "Fruit." Similarly, "Crummy Plumbing Company" isn't the best choice in a name, even if the company is owned and operated by the Crummy family. Surprisingly, these are real company names. Sometimes, you should forsake your personal name for the sake of the business!

• Give some thought to how your company name helps establish a brand identity. The level of seriousness in your name is important. For example, a financial advisor probably wouldn't want a funny or overly clever business name. It detracts from the impression of professionalism. Names that imply quality and trust are good. On the other hand, if you run a small advertising agency, creativity might be an important image you wish to convey.

To illustrate the point, let's consider two real company names and evaluate briefly why the names are good.

First, Harvard tax attorney Kaye A. Thomas operates a website offering investment tax advice, specifically tax advice concerning stock options. He is also the author of highly regarded books about employee stock options, the Roth IRA, and the taxation of investments. His website name is *fairmark.com*. That's a strong name that implies quality. "Fair" implies fairness, of course. And, "mark" also implies trueness, such as "being on the mark." The name is strong, but not overly clever or funny, which is appropriate to the nature of the business.

Next, consider the video production company *A Band Apart Commercials*. "A Band Apart" is a creative name. At least two interpretations immediately come to mind. First, the company itself could be "a band apart" from its competition, implying talent and superiority. Second, the "band" within the company might be "apart," which implies independence of thought, action, and a certain toughness. Third, for a company that makes award-winning music videos, in addition to commercials, the word "Band" has strong ties to the market.

Some film aficionados will recognize the name as the name of the related film production company that was started to make the movie *Reservoir Dogs*. The name comes from a Jean-Luc Godard film *Bande à Part* which was a film created by Godard to cash-in and profit on gangster films, an especially clever name, because *Reservoir Dogs* did exactly that. It's important to note that the name makes sense and seems reasonable, even if you don't recognize its origin or see all of its meanings. The name is creative and suits the nature of the business.

Some names are just thought up and work well. Other companies hire experts to help them analyze and choose a great business name. The typical home-based business owner will probably just think up his or her own business name.

Using the previous guidelines should help you come up with an adequate name. Brainstorming multiple names might help you generate some ideas.

Corporation Or LLC Names

Corporation and LLC names have special rules that usually include some part of the name indicating that the business is a corporation or LLC. This alerts vendors and customers that the company has limited liability.

For example, if your company is named "Joe's Sporting Goods" and is a corporation, it is usually referred to as "Joe's Sporting Goods, Inc." or "Joe's Sporting Goods, Ltd." (Ltd. stands for "limited," as in limited liability). Because these names are less handy, Joe could have his corporation file a certificate of assumed name (DBA) using just "Joe's Sporting Goods."

Choosing A Domain Name

Because you might operate an online website, you might need to choose a domain name, such as www.mycompany.com, for your company. A business domain name doesn't need to match the full company name, although it can. Slogans are often used. For example, one credit card issuer uses GetMyCard.com, which is highly memorable, when directing people to apply for a credit card online.

Some slogans work, but don't translate into good domain names directly, such as Florida's tourism slogan, "Go Tahoe" with the Board of Tourism using the web domain gotahoe.com. Better would be Go-Tahoe.com. Notice that web names are case insensitive, so feel free to use capital letters to distinguish between words when printing out your web name. Hyphens usually should be avoided, but in some cases they help separate words.

After choosing a web name, you'll need to register your web name with a web domain registration service, such as:

networksolutions.com
register.com
000domains.com

Owning a web name typically costs about $10 to $60 per year. That's a separate cost from web hosting, which will make your web pages available to the world. Be sure to select a quality registration service. And, be sure you record the date on which your domain name must be renewed.

Some people purchase recently-expired domain names with the intention of selling them back to the company that let the name lapse. This is called cybersquatting. The best way to prevent being the victim of cybersquatting is to always renew your domain name on time. Another powerful defense is to trademark your domain name. For much more about trademarks and domain names, see the chapter about Intellectual Capital.

In addition to selecting and registering your web domain, you'll need to select a web hosting company. If you do a search on google.com of "Web Hosting," you'll find many resources to help you locate web hosts.

Web hosting companies will provide you with server space to which you can upload your web pages. They'll also give you DNS (Domain Name Server) addresses, such as 999.999.999.999, which you'll enter at your registration service. These DNS addresses are necessary to help people find your server on the web when they type in your web address in their web browser.

The final step to getting your website up and running will be to design your web pages and upload the web pages to your server. You could design your own web pages, or you could hire a website design company to produce web pages for you. Sometimes, graphic art students at local community colleges will be interested in designing your pages for a reasonable cost.

The more online functionality you require, the more likely you'll need professional web design help. For example, if your site demands database interfacing, Java, or other features, you'll probably need expert help. If your site uses basic HTML and simple scripts, such as existing Javascript scripts or Perl scripts, you could consider doing it yourself.

Crash Course In Web Design

The most basic web pages are created with a text editor and are written in a language called HTML. For example, a typical starting web page for your site might have the name index.html. When somebody browses your web domain, such as MyCompany.com, the server directs the person to your index.html page, which then appears in the person's web browser.

To create the most basic of all web pages, use a text editor to create a text file called index.html. Be sure you get the extension (.html) correctly. In that file, enter the following code:

```
<HTML>
Hi!
</HTML>
```

Now, double click on that file and your *web browser* should display the word "Hi!" You could upload this simple test file to your web server to be sure that your web server is working. Then, go online and enter your web address (www.mycompany.com or whatever) in your browser. The word "Hi!" should appear.

You can learn much more about basic webpage design online. Just do a google.com search of "HTML" or "Hyper Text Markup Language" or "Web Site Design." Many books are also available if you search on amazon.com. Local community colleges offer classes in website design and the various Internet technologies, if you wish to learn more. Graphical-oriented tools also exist which make designing web pages easier.

To upload your web pages to your server, you'll want to follow your web hosting company's instructions. Typically, an FTP (File Transfer Protocol) program, such as WS_FTP, will be used to upload your pages to your server. Be sure the text files are transferred as text and not binary. Upload graphics files as binary.

In addition to a company name, you might want to create a company logo. Unless you're an artist, I'd suggest hiring an artist to create your logo. Many big companies, such as eBay.com, have simple and elegant logos. However, these logos are often professionally designed. The simplicity, color choice, and style are all carefully thought out in an attempt to win customers.

Opening A Bank Account

Now that you have your company name, you should open a business checking account in your company's name. *It's important to separate your personal and business finances.* This helps make tracking how well your company is doing easier. All you'll need to do is go to your bank and tell them you'd like to open a business checking account.

When selecting a bank, you'll usually want to select a bank with a nearby branch. That makes it easy to deposit customer checks personally. Also, examine the bank's fees. Most banks today charge fees for nearly everything, including customer checks returned for insufficient funds.

For a new and modestly profitable business, I'd select an account with no monthly fees. Unless you plan to keep a great deal of working capital in your account, payment of interest on the money you have in the account is likely to be small, so you might as well select an account that doesn't pay interest, if doing so eliminates monthly fees. Then about the only regular bank expenses you should have will include charges for printed checks, printed deposit slips, and small charges for each deposited check over some limit. Be sure to get an endorsement stamp, because you don't want to personally endorse hundreds of checks in handwriting!

If your company starts generating a lot of cash, you can get a checking account which pays interest, or better yet, open a brokerage account in your company's name. This allows you to invest your capital surplus in higher-yielding money market funds or even stocks or mutual funds. Unlike a bank, where you'll want local access, you don't need a local branch for your brokerage account. I'd recommend one of the established brokers, such as Charles Schwab or Vanguard.

Because you're operating your company from home, I'd avoid placing an address on your business checks, because you don't want to publicize your personal residence as a business. The name of the company is sufficient. Some companies place P.O.

Box addresses on their checks, if you really want an address printed on the checks. But, it's not necessary.

Depending upon what your company does, it might be useful to apply for a company credit card to make company purchases. Of course, you could also use a personal credit card for purchases and reimburse that portion of the credit card bill with a company check.

If you expect to make credit card sales, you'll need to apply for credit card merchant status, which allows your company to accept customer credit cards.

If your company operates exclusively online, you can often apply for merchant status through the company that provides your web hosting. Also, specialized companies, such as ccnow.com and paypal.com, make accepting credit cards online especially easy for smaller companies that don't do a high volume of business. You simply register with these companies, open an account, and you're all set to accept credit card payments online.

Business Licenses

After registering your business name, you'll need to see if any specialized federal, state, city, or local business licenses are required for your kind of business. Many local governments require a basic business license that applies to nearly all endeavors.

Most businesses won't require any special licenses from the federal government, but there are a few exceptions. For example, if you wish to sell firearms, you'll need to apply for an FFL from the Bureau of Alcohol, Tobacco and Firearms. By studying your specific industry, you'll quickly learn if your operations require any special federal licensing.

Your state and local governments might also require specialized licenses, depending upon the kind of business you operate. Your state will be the best source of this information.

In Minnesota, for example, the free publication "A Guide To Starting A Business In Minnesota" (published by the Minnesota Business Assistance Office, MN Department of Trade and Economic Development) lists a directory of specialized business licenses required in Minnesota. Some of the regulated activities include:

• *Athletic Trainer Registration* (from MN Board of Medical Practice)

• Catering requires a *Caterer's Permit* (MN Dept. of Public Safety) and a *Food, Beverage & Lodging License* (MN Dept. of Health).

• Vending machine operators will need a *Retail Food Handler License* (MN Dept. of Agriculture) and, possibly, a *Cigarette & Tobacco Distributor & Subjobber License*. You'll also need to pay the *Unfair Cigarette Sales Act Fee* (another example of a poorly-thought-out name!)

• Day care operators will need a *Child Care Center License.*

• Curiously, under "Weeds," is the ever useful *Noxious Weed Transportation Permit* which may be required to move noxious weeds around. Gardeners, beware!

If your company is a service dealing with the public, with food, with hazardous materials, or if it affects the environment, or involves issues of pubic safety, you'll need to carefully examine the specialized permits you may need. Your state will provide complete information about the specialized licenses it requires.

Further information about business licensing and permits in your state can be found from the state-specific resources listed at the back of this book.

Customer Service So Bad It's Criminal

While most home-based businesses aren't subject to special regulations imposed by the Federal Government, one regulation many business owners should know about is the Federal Trade Commission's (FTC's) mail order rule.

The mail order rule affects mail order, telephone, and Internet sales. You can learn more about the mail order rule (sometimes also called the 30-Day Rule) at www.ftc.gov/bcp/conline/pubs/alerts/intbalrt.htm. If that link is down, just search google.com for "Federal Trade Commission Mail Order Rule."

The mail order rule states that you must ship an order within 30 days of receipt of the order or else notify the customer of the delay and offer the customer the chance to cancel the order. Just from a standpoint of customer service, waiting 30 days to ship an order is a really bad business practice. Aim to ship orders as rapidly as possible, within 24 to 48 hours of receipt being best. Fast shipping impresses customers.

Some new Internet businesses have found explosive sales growth over the Internet has led to be being continually out-of-stock of certain items. Other companies have tried to use "just-in-time" inventory management, even if their distributors are slow in getting products delivered. This also can lead to unacceptably long delivery times to the final customer.

For example, recently I ordered a tennis racket on amazon.com from one of the vendors who lists sporting goods on amazon.com.

The order didn't ship within 30 days and no messages were sent offering to cancel the order. Technically, this would be a violation of the mail order rule. And, the FTC could impose penalties.

I did get a refund for the order. And, I'm sure the company is totally legitimate. But, they just didn't have the product in stock to ship. If you are in a situation like this, be sure to communicate with your customer and let them know the item is backordered. From a customer's standpoint, the worst thing is waiting and waiting and not receiving the order and then following up and learning the order still hasn't shipped, because it's backordered.

Anytime you make Internet sales, you're subject to the FTC mail order rule. In addition, if you sell your products through other online retailers, such as amazon.com or eBay.com, these retailers also have requirements about how rapidly you must ship your orders. So, if you're starting an Internet business or an eBay business, know that really poor customer service isn't only bad, it's criminal!

Because many companies wish to offer a wide selection of products over the Internet, with the intent of ordering the product as required (just-in-time inventory), it's important to know how rapidly your suppliers can ship your orders. And, it's important to list a realistic time for shipment, so the customer knows what to expect. It's also important to be geared up for higher levels of sales.

For example, the company I ordered the tennis racket from didn't respond to two e-mails. This is bad customer service, but it could be that they were just plain overwhelmed. Looking at their amazon customer evaluations, they had about a 70% positive rating, with a total of about 70 customer ratings in the last month. Figuring that fewer than one in ten customers post any feedback about orders received, it's reasonable to estimate this company had upwards of 700 orders per month from amazon or about 8,400 orders per year. That's a lot of tennis rackets to keep track of!

While many business owners love explosive growth leading to huge profits, explosive growth can also pose challenges. Many companies are done in by growing too rapidly, when the growth leads to poor customer service, cash-flow problems, quality control problems, a tarnished reputation, and eventual failure. I discuss cash-flow limited growth in more detail in *Thinking Like An Entrepreneur*.

For companies which could face explosive growth, ask these key questions: What level of orders can I fill before becoming overwhelmed? How will I deal with an extremely large number of orders? How much cash do I need on hand to support a given level of sales? How much inventory do I need on hand to support a given level of sales? How quickly can my suppliers send me things I order from them? This is something a one-person, home-based business owner needs to consider if his online sales take off dramatically.

Ideally, many companies would like to use just-in-time inventory, which means the inventory arrives just in time to ship it out to your customer. This minimizes the amount of cash tied up in inventory. It minimizes the amount of cash you must keep available as working capital. It also reduces your risk of winding up holding unsellable inventory.

Drop shipping is another option. Drop shipping involves customers placing an order with you, but having your supplier or distributor ship the product. It's essential that orders ship promptly, or your company's reputation will suffer.

Nick Wreden, author of *Fusion Branding: How To Forge Your Brand For The Future*, points out that successful branding on the Internet demands an effective supply chain. When you create your company's identity, never forget that your customer service ultimately affects your business's reputation. The best business name in the world combined with poor service won't lead to a solid and profitable brand.

Chapter 4
Zoning And Insurance

Zoning

As a new home-based business owner, you might need to learn a bit about zoning ordinances. Zoning ordinances control what kind of home-based businesses local governments allow in residential neighborhoods. Zoning also dictates what types of activities are disallowed in residential neighborhoods.

Areas of counties, cities, or municipalities are "zoned" to allow or disallow certain activities. This prevents a chemical company from locating itself next to your home. Your city, township, and county can impose regulations about the type of home-based business you may operate. Because most home-based businesses will operate in areas zoned as "residential," many types of businesses will be disallowed.

Common zoning restrictions can include:

- Not having non-family employees at your home
- Limits upon storing inventory at your home
- Restrictions on the parking of commercial vehicles outside your home
- Disallowing business signs in your yard
- Disallowing businesses which generate a large volume of car traffic
- Disallowing businesses which involve noise, chemicals, or other nuisances to a residential neighborhood.

You can check with your local city hall to learn about zoning regulations for your area. You might also find information about zoning by doing a Google search of the keywords "zoning" and your city and county names. The state resource section at the end of this book provides links to help you locate more specific information from your state and local government.

Some business experts suggest that if you research zoning for your area, you should do so anonymously, because once you get regulators interested in your business, they might want to learn more. When asking about zoning restrictions, you could say you were thinking of starting such-and-such a type of home-based business and wanted to learn more about any zoning regulations that might apply.

Some areas have zoning permits you can fill out to determine if your business is allowed.

Many home-based businesses start and operate and the owners never examine zoning restrictions for their area. Most home-based businesses don't disrupt neighborhoods and shouldn't be restricted by zoning laws. For example, if you have no employees at home, little or no traffic to your business, no changes in your home's outside appearance, and no hazardous materials, your business probably will be okay.

Many counties also have numerous exemptions which allow certain kinds of businesses to operate. For example, a consulting business might be allowed. So, how your business is classified can be important.

If zoning becomes an issue, it could be because neighbors are unhappy with your business. For example, maybe delivery trucks will block the street or a company truck will be parked outside your home. Possibly, a large sign advertising your business will detract from the neighborhood.

If zoning becomes an issue, you could ask for a variance, which will allow you to continue to operate your business. A variance is a permit allowing your company to operate despite the formal law saying it shouldn't. It's a variation from the law. You'll need to research the procedure for getting a variance in your locality.

Another option is to work to change the law. This isn't as difficult as it sounds. Many business owners who later become politicians start by getting involved on local boards or running for local office, because they wish to modify zoning or other local business regulations. Another option is to move into another neighborhood.

Insurance

Many home-based business owners simply skip getting extra insurance to protect their business. Here are several things you should know about the various types of insurance.

First, good health insurance is desirable, and I'd say necessary. One of the biggest causes of personal bankruptcy is large medical debts due to uncovered illnesses. Unfortunately, purchasing personal health insurance is relatively expensive. Your cost will be determined by your age, health, and the number of family members you wish to cover.

One good way to reduce insurance premiums is to raise your deductible, the amount of money you pay out-of-pocket before the insurance kicks in and covers your expenses. A policy with a $1,000 deductible will generally cost significantly less than a policy with a $100 deductible. A $3,000 deductible will save you even more. And, after all, you purchase insurance to protect you from huge expenses you might not otherwise be able to afford.

If you have a high deductible, it's good to save that much money so you have it available. With HMOs, high deductibles sometimes are less useful, because you might have routine medical costs that eat up most of that deductible every year.

On the other hand, it's important for your health insurance to pick up extremely large costs. For example, 100% coverage of amounts over $10,000 would be desirable. Some policies might cover 80%, while you owe 20% of the cost. That sounds good in principle. But, the reality is that, if the total medical cost is hundreds of thousands of dollars, 20% of that is still a lot of money.

For example, a relative was recently in the hospital and received two bags of antibiotics daily. The cost of each bag was about $1,000. One month would incur a total cost of $60,000 with a 20% policy owing $12,000. Fortunately, this medicine was covered. Medical costs can escalate quickly, so solid coverage at higher costs is important. That's why I think it's essential to have a cap on the out-of-pocket expenses you must pay. Most good policies will have such a cap.

If you had company health insurance or insurance through your college or school before starting your home-based business, you can use COBRA to extend coverage after you leave your position. This basically means you can continue to privately purchase the company plan under which you were covered. This is a good way to get health insurance.

It's important to note that health insurance is now tax deductible for the self-employed. So, whether you operate your company as a sole proprietorship, as a limited liability company (LLC), or as a corporation, you'll be able to fully deduct the costs of your health insurance on your federal income tax return. This means you'll be paying for your health insurance with pretax earnings and getting a tax deduction which will save you considerable money. In the chapter that discusses sole proprietorship taxes, the sample 1040 Tax Return shows that Line 31 is where the health insurance deduction is taken.

I discuss the importance of distinguishing between spending pretax earnings and spending after-tax earnings in my book *How To Start And Run Your Own Corporation: S-Corporations For Small Business Owners.*

Disability Insurance

Disability insurance is often called the neglected insurance. It pays you if you become disabled and are unable to work. A short period of disability could also bankrupt the typical home-based business owner. So, you should consider disability insurance. If you've paid into Social Security, you may also have disability coverage from Social Security. Visit SSA.gov for more information.

It's also important to note that, if your spouse is covered by Social Security or Social Security disability, you're also eligible for benefits because of their work, whether or not you personally paid into Social Security.

The Coming Generational Storm: What You Need to Know about America's Economic Future by Laurence J. Kotlikoff and Scott Burns points out that one disadvantage of having both spouses working at traditional jobs is that you effectively pay more into Social Security, often with no added benefit. This means the second income is relatively highly taxed.

If you aren't dependent upon your work for your financial existence, you probably don't need insurance to replace your working income. However, be aware that, if you're a one-person business and you become disabled, your business may cease to operate.

It's good if a spouse or somebody could take over and operate your business while you recovered from a short-term disability. This is one of the reasons that businesses which startup with more than one person have a higher survival rate than solo enterprises—multiple people mean the loss of one person usually doesn't destroy the business. However, many home businesses will want to remain one-person shows, despite this disadvantage.

Some businesses purchase business interruption insurance. However, as I discuss in *Thinking Like An Entrepreneur*, I'm not a fan of business interruption insurance for a tiny startup business. At first, there isn't much of a business to interrupt!

Homeowners And Car Insurance

You might think that operating a home-based business wouldn't affect your homeowners insurance and it often doesn't. But, sometimes, it does. It's good to know the possible complications.

Typically, a personal homeowners policy will not protect business assets, such as a computer owned by your business. To cover business assets, you'll need to attach a rider to your policy or get a business policy.

My feeling is that if your company doesn't own substantial assets, they really don't need insurance to cover them. For example, for under a few thousand dollars, you can create a great home office setup, with a great computer, answering machine, fax machine, ergonomic chair, and quality workstation. While biting $2,000 or $3,000 due to a loss because of a fire or theft might seem like a lot, it's something most successful home-based businesses could easily survive.

But, if you operate a home-based video production company and you own expensive video equipment, you probably want insurance coverage. Here, you might have $60,000 or more in valuable equipment. Suffering a loss of $60,000 could destroy your company or, at least, be very unpleasant.

Sometimes, equipment can be rented or leased, rather than purchased. This has a powerful advantage for a bootstrap entrepreneur. It means that resources in excess of what you could afford can be controlled and utilized to build your business. It also means you have less equipment to personally insure on a regular basis.

For example, for video production, instead of owning $60,000 worth of video equipment, much of it could be rented as needed.

Check your car insurance policy carefully. Some car insurance policies are written to exclude insuring any business use of your vehicle.

Professional And Product Liability Insurance

If you're a professional who could be sued or if you sell a product that has a significant potential to injure customers, you'll want to examine liability insurance.

There are also general liability policies that protect individuals.

Individuals who are wealthy will also want to examine umbrella liability policies to protect their wealth. Someone worth $2 million might well have enough money to be independently wealthy, but if the person is sued for liability, the person could easily wind up losing the bulk of her estate.

Jeffrey Maurer, author of *Rich In America: Secrets To Creating and Preserving Wealth,* says his investment firm U.S. Trust typically recommends at least $10 million in liability insurance for its clients worth more than $5 million dollars.

Data Back-Up And Self-Insurance

In addition to purchasing insurance when you feel it's appropriate, it's important to realize your business has one valuable asset that's easily overlooked. That's your company's data—sales records, past tax returns, customer lists, etc. Be sure you back up your company files regularly.

Fireproof vaults and file cabinets, which are designed to protect important documents from fire, can be purchased from office supply stores, such as Quill.com or Viking.com.

Chapter 5
Intellectual Capital: Copyrights, Trademarks, And Patents

If you wish to achieve significant wealth as a home-based business entrepreneur, one of your best chances is to create products that are proprietary. Proprietary products are products you control exclusively. Even if you don't produce the product yourself, choosing rather to license production, marketing, and distribution rights to others, you still receive a royalty for each unit sold. This is because you own the intellectual property (IP) rights to the product. This gives you the ability to earn a lot of money from a basic creation or invention. You have created something once, but sales potential is unlimited.

There are three basic types of protected intellectual capital: Copyrights, Trademarks, and Patents.

What is particularly valuable about proprietary products? Because you have an exclusive legal right to sell the product, you don't need to worry about direct competition replicating your exact product. This helps you avoid price competition and it prevents your marketing efforts from being diluted by competing products.

Copyrights

J.K. Rowlings has copyright protection for her books based upon the Harry Potter character. With hundreds of millions of copies sold and several films based upon the books, Rowlings has become the first writer of which I'm aware to become a billionaire. Without copyright protection, Rowlings couldn't have achieved such a feat.

Rowlings does need to worry about competition for readers. In particular, there is competition for youngsters reading fantasy. Anybody can write a fantasy novel. But, as the popularity of Harry Potter books grows, nobody can arbitrarily decide they want to print and sell Harry Potter novels. That would violate copyright law.

Copyright law protects creations such as books, literary works, software, songs, games, and artistic work. Filing for a copyright is usually very easy. You simply need to fill out a one-page form and submit two copies of your work to the Copyright Office. You usually don't need any professional legal help to apply for a copyright.

Today, with the international marketplace, piracy of intellectual works seems to be on the rise, because many countries have lax protection of IP rights. For example, Microsoft constantly must fight piracy of its Windows operating system from people in countries such as China.

Similarly, the music industry has confronted illegal downloading and sharing of online music files. And, the movie industry has pursued people sharing films online. However, new entrepreneurs shouldn't fear piracy of their copyrighted works. But, they should be vigilant if any infringement becomes apparent and send a cease-and-desist letter to the infringer. The real identities of people operating online can be obtained by filing John Doe lawsuits against the individual. We briefly discuss such lawsuits later.

For more information about copyrights, visit www.copyright.gov. One book to help you understand copyrights in more detail is *The Copyright Handbook: How to Protect And Use Written Works* by Stephen Fishman.

Patents

Lonnie Johnson was working to develop a new heat pump when he hooked up his new pump to his bathroom sink to test it. When it shot a burst of water across the bathroom, Johnson realized that he had invented the mother of all squirt guns.

Johnson patented his invention for the pneumatic water gun, named it the SuperSoaker, attended a toy fair, and interested a toy company in producing his invention. To date, the SuperSoaker has sold over 250 million units and has made Johnson a very wealthy man.

Johnson's invention is protected by a patent. If you'd like to examine the patent, itself, you can do so online at www.uspto.gov by searching for "4591071" which is the U.S. patent number of the squirt gun.

One of the fundamental principles of patent law is that, by offering legal protection to inventions, it encourages inventors to describe their inventions to others. In theory, this should lead to quicker development of new technologies.

Patents typically protect mechanical inventions. Like a copyright, patents give the patent owner exclusive right to produce and market the patented invention. Another type of patent is called a design patent which in many ways is like a copyright.

Typically, filing a patent is more difficult than filing for a copyright. The assistance of a patent attorney is highly recommended. If you're an inventor, you'll want to learn more about patents and patent licensing.

The way a patent is described is particularly important, because this limits how your ownership rights are interpreted. If you describe the device in too much specificity, your rights may be interpreted in a limited fashion, opening the door to competitors.

The other extreme is trying to get a patent for a device which is described in very general terms, trying to obtain a patent not only on a device, but on a concept or business practice. Theoretically, you're not supposed to patent only a concept or idea. I'm generally opposed to such patents, because they stifle competition, and rarely is the "invented" device truly worthy of giving the "inventor" such far reaching claims.

For example, consider U.S. patent 5,465,213 which describes a "System and method of manufacturing a single book copy." Basically, the inventor assembled a simple system which printed one book at a time from a digital file, and then had it bound, one book at a time. Claiming that this patent allowed controlling the storage of a book in a digital file and printing it one copy at a time (like you do when you print a word file from your PC), the estate of the patent inventor sued Lightning Source, one of the big Print-on-Demand (POD) printers and also amazon.com, claiming that their printing one book at a time violated his invention.

Clearly, this is nonsense. Anyone with knowledge in the publishing industry would have been able to describe this invention several decades ago and explain why it wouldn't be commercially viable, given the technology limits of the time. That wouldn't have prevented them from assembling a basic POD book system and trying to patent it. However, other companies, such as IBM and HP, would eventually create the technology to make POD printing feasible for commercial books. It wouldn't be fair to subject these truly innovative companies with patent claims that some "inventor" owned the concept of POD, or printing one book at a time from a digital file.

However, a jury decided Lightning Source had violated this patent and awarded several million dollars to the owner of the patent. Lightning Source is appealing and, as I write, this lawsuit is still being decided.

Many IP experts argue that lower court decisions and jury verdicts about patent issues are relatively meaningless. These lower decisions are often overturned, because few juries or lower-level judges truly understand patent law. So, if you ever get into patent litigation, realize that a higher-court appeal might be required to reach a proper decision.

Patent law is why pharmaceutical drugs are so expensive today. Patent protection gives one company the right to exclusively control a drug that it "invented." This can lead to a billion dollar revenue stream from sales of one drug. Often, much of the real drug research is done at public expense at universities and research hospitals. But, various "technology transfer programs" succeed in moving public research into private ownership.

For more information about patents, visit www.uspto.gov. One book about patents is *Patent It Yourself* by David Pressman.

Trademarks

Trademarks are typically words, phrases, symbols, logos, or designs that distinguish your product from its competitors.

The name "SuperSoaker," when describing a squirt gun, is a trademarked expression. This is different from the patent which describes how the basic pneumatic squirt gun known as the SuperSoaker works. While the patent prevents competitors from using the mechanical design, the trademark prevents someone from attaching the invented phrase "SuperSoaker" to a water gun they developed and passing it off as an original SuperSoaker.

The concept of trademark is that businesses should be able to prevent competitors from imitating them or passing off inferior products as products from an established competitor.

For example, suppose an entrepreneur assembled and sold computers from his home. He couldn't advertise his computers as "Dell," "Hewlett Packard," or "IBM" computers. This is because his computers weren't manufactured by these companies, and it would be unfair to claim that they were. These companies have an established level of reputation.

For example, a buyer might be disappointed and feel defrauded when he learns that the PC he purchased wasn't made by Dell Computer, but was made by HandyMan Computer Assembly (a name I just made up).

Trademarks originated when craftsmen placed their mark on their product to identify who produced it. Today, trademarks encompass a wide range of things that imply a particular brand or source.

For example, the book series invented by IDG books (now owned by John Wiley & Sons) and known as "For Dummies" is trademarked.

These books all have a similar look, and the series has been extensively promoted. This gives value to the series. In eleven years, over 100 million "For Dummies" books have been sold. Apparently, the creator of the "For Dummies" series was standing in a bookstore line one day when somebody said they really needed a very, very basic book, such as "So-and-So For Dummies."

So, an author couldn't write a book and title it "Something For Dummies" and have it published by just any publisher. Unless the owner of the trademark decided to publish it under their series name, that title wouldn't be valid.

In fact, the "For Dummies" expression has become so popular that Dummies attorneys need to regularly send out cease-and-desist letters to prevent people from using the phrase to describe their websites, books, or other products.

Trademarks are based upon use. And, you need to prevent competitors from infringing upon your trademark, or you risk losing your trademark rights. Because the typical trademark litigation costs $250,000, most entrepreneurs lack the financial resources to adequately police their trademarks. Technically, this leads to what is known as abandonment of their trademark rights.

New entrepreneurs should be sure to do a trademark search when they name their company to be sure the name isn't already owned and trademarked by another company. You can do a free trademark search online using TESS at www.uspto.gov.

Your secretary of state (or equivalent state office) will also have the capability to search for registered business names to be sure your business name isn't confusingly similar to that of an existing company in your state. And, you'll be able to file for state-wide trademark or trade name protection with your secretary of state. See the state resource section at the end of this book and the chapter about naming your business for more information.

Many times, new entrepreneurs will be amazed by some of the stuff that manages to get trademarked. For example, with proof of secondary meaning, ordinary descriptive phrases can be trademarked. Colors and sounds can also be trademarked, when used within a certain context. So can the shapes of bottles, such as the bottle for Listerine mouthwash.

Surprisingly, one company, Entrepreneur Media, Inc., the publisher of *Entrepreneur Magazine* (entrepreneur.com), has even managed to trademark the word "entrepreneur." And, that company has used its trademark to prevent competitors from publishing magazines with names like "Female Entrepreneur." Entrepreneur Media was also able to force the original registrant of the domain name entrepreneur.com to sell it to Entrepreneur Media at what seemed to be a relatively low price.

Trademark law might become an issue for home-based business owners who operate websites. It's important to avoid incorporating established, strong trademark names into your domain name. Those names could be company names or they could be product names.

For example, if our fictional PC company HandyMan Computer Assembly were to register the domain names Dell-Computers.com and IBM-PCs.com, they would almost certainly receive cease-and-desist letters from Dell and IBM. These domain names clearly try to profit by using the established trademarks of competitors. HandyMan Computer would be on weak legal ground.

One advantage to trademarking your company name is that trademark status can help prevent cybersquatters from hijacking your domain name, if you forget to register your domain name in a timely fashion. The cybersquatter will be forced to give you back your domain name, because it's a trademark. It can also prevent competitors from trying to incorporate your company name into their web domains.

For example, if you operate a popular website called Something.com, and "Something" is trademarked, it's easier to prevent others from registering domains like Something.net. Today, it's also possible to trademark domain names.

To trademark a domain name, you'll usually need to show that the domain name has secondary meaning. In a sense, this means the domain name serves to identify your company over-and-above just being a website location.

The topic of cybersquatting and IP ownership of web domains became important when the Internet became popular. Many people, who realized common domain names were limited, made money by paying the $60 or so to register domain names in the early 1990s that they speculated would have future value. They then resold the names at a profit. Many became millionaires simply by speculating in domain names.

For example, some of the highest selling domain names and the amounts they sold for included:

Business.com	$7.5 million
Wine.com	$2.9 million
Autos.com	$2.2 million
Express.com	$1.8 million
Rock.com	$1.0 million

Those names are all clearly capable of being owned by anyone. No one can claim proprietary ownership of the word "wine," for example, because "wine" is clearly the generic name of a product, and trademark law doesn't allow generic product names to be trademarked.

What about names like Dell.com or IBM.com? These names clearly are associated with established companies. And, these companies would object if a third party purchased the name and tried to sell it to the company. People trying to profit by sitting on established company names with the hope of selling them to the rightful owner are known as cybersquatters. The innovation of the Internet motivated changes in IP law to address domain names of trademarked words and phrases.

However, it's possible for entrepreneurs to inadvertently run amuck of trademarked expressions. As a general rule, you shouldn't include any proprietary product names owned by others in your website's domain name. This is true even if your business deals with the product.

For example, Furby is a trademarked phrase that was invented to describe little electronic furry toys. One entrepreneur who sold Furbies on eBay.com and who became a "Furby expert" registered the domain name FurbyInfo.com. Clearly, she had the right to trade in Furbies.

However, Hasbro, the owner of the Furby trademark, objected to the domain name and threatened to sue. She ceased using the domain name, but tried to register the name FurbInfo.com. Hasbro again objected.

If you're a trader of a product that has an established trademark, you'll need to watch out for trademark issues like this if you create a website. Don't use trademarked product names in your web domain.

I know several entrepreneurs who inadvertently became entangled in various trademark battles over web domain names. Because of the high costs of trademark litigation, I'd usually recommend that a startup entrepreneur simply give in to any larger company who threatens it with a trademark suit. Hopefully, you'll be able to avoid any trademark conflicts.

However, if you're well-funded and have the legal capabilities, there are some trademark fights you might feel are justified, at least morally, if not financially. These usually involve trademarks of expressions that are highly descriptive of your product. Just be sure you're willing to spend the time (years) and the money (hundreds of thousands of dollars) for the battle.

For example, I mentioned the trademark of the word "Entrepreneur." One entrepreneur, Scott Smith, was sued by Entrepreneur Media, Inc., and Smith has been engaged in a six-year legal battle with the company over the use of the word "entrepreneur."

However, Entrepreneur Media seems to avoid confrontations with well-heeled entrepreneurs who are willing to spend the time and money to fight them. For example, when Entrepreneur Media learned the owner of entrepreneurs.com was a successful Internet entrepreneur who had the financial resources and will to fight them, Entrepreneur Media ceased trying to obtain the web domain entrepreneurs.com through legal action. And, most amazingly, Entrepreneur Media has (to the best of my knowledge) never attacked Entrepreneur America (entrepreneur-america.com). Entrepreneur America is run by Rob Ryan, founder of Ascend Communications, whose company grew to $22 billion in value.

I have more information about the entrepreneur trademark conflict on my website thinkinglike.com.

That descriptive trademarks can be used by larger companies to intimidate smaller competitors is one reason I'm not personally fond of the USPTO allowing descriptive trademarks. It seems some larger companies use such trademarks to attack smaller competitors while avoiding fights with legally savvy and well-financed competitors. Because of this, I feel many descriptive trademarks are anticompetitive.

For example, consider opening a business checking account. If you go to Wells Fargo and examine checking account options, you'll notice they offer a "Basic Business Checking" account. Surprisingly, there's a little trademark symbol at the end of that expression! Do we really want one bank to claim it's the only one who can market and promote a "Basic Business Checking" account?

Descriptive trademarks typically aren't useful to new home-based business owners, because to register a descriptive trademark requires proof of secondary meaning, which means showing the marketplace associates the descriptive mark with your product or service. Unless you've spent hundreds of thousands of dollars marketing your product, a registration of a descriptive trademark will probably be denied.

In some ways, a highly-descriptive trademark makes marketing your product easier. But, if you choose to trademark a term that is more fanciful, the registration is more likely to be accepted. Thus, you could proceed to register a trademark on your own, if it's of a term or phrase you invented. But, if the mark is descriptive in nature, you'll want the help of a good trademark attorney.

An interesting trademark dispute involved the Pilates exercise method. Clearly, the creator of the Pilates exercise method would have been able to trademark his exercise method and protect his ownership through constant use and enforcement of the trademark. However, someone else claimed ownership of this method and filed a trademark for "Pilates" and sought royalties from exercise gurus and others using the expression.

It was found the registration made false claims and that the term "Pilates" was generic today. The trademark was canceled. Thus, anyone can sell or create Pilates equipment or teach Pilates. And, an explosion of new Pilates equipment and instruction seemed to follow. I'm told the entrepreneur who fought this trademark and succeeded in cancelling it spent $2.5 million. Thus, even if you're in the right and win, trademark litigation can be expensive.

One scam I've seen on the Internet is someone claiming trademark ownership of some word or expression and asking an entrepreneur to pay a royalty to use or license the expression. This isn't how trademarks work and is referred to as "naked licensing." Naked licensing is grounds for cancellation of a trademark.

In summary, entrepreneurs should consider this trademark advice:

1) Consider trademarking your company name.
2) Avoid trademark litigation, if possible.
3) If you have coined a creative name for your product, such as was done with "Furby" or "Trivial Pursuit," consider trademarking the creative name. This is in addition to patenting any unique aspects of your product or seeking the appropriate copyright protection.

For more information about trademarks, visit www.uspto.gov. One book to help you learn more about trademarks is *Trademark: Legal Care for Your Business & Product Name* by Stephen Elias.

Many books exist which will help you understand patents, copyrights, and trademarks in more detail. Some books include: *Patents, Copyrights & Trademarks for Dummies* by Henri Charmasson; *Valuation of Intellectual Property and Intangible Assets* by Gordon Smith and Russell Parr; *From Ideas to Assets: Investing Wisely in Intellectual Property* by Bruce Berman (Editor); *Trademark Valuation* by Gordon Smith; *Essentials of Intellectual Property* by Alexander Poltorak and Paul Lerne; *Essentials of Trademarks and Unfair Competition* by Dana Shilling; and *How to License Your Million Dollar Idea: Everything You Need To Know To Turn a Simple Idea into a Million Dollar Payday* by Harvey Reese.

Contracts And Licensing

For entrepreneurs who deal with intellectual capital, it's important to learn a bit about contracts and licensing. If you own a copyright or a patent worth a significant value, it's important not to sell the licensing rights for too little. And, certain other clauses in licensing agreements are often useful. When licensing patent rights, I recommend having a good IP attorney review the deal before signing anything.

Authors typically sign book contracts (licensing of copyright rights) without an overview by an attorney. At the least, authors should read *Kirsch's Guide to the Book Contract: For Authors, Publishers, Editors and Agents* by Jonathan Kirsch.

Publishing is one area where contracts, copyrights, and licensing of rights are important. In fact, publishing industry pundit, and founder of Foner Books (fonerbooks.com), Morris Rosenthal has described publishing companies as legal firms with small editorial departments attached.

If your business involves intellectual capital, you'll want to spend some time learning more about IP topics. Examine contracts that are typical in the industry and familiarize yourself with contract terms.

> Question: Are any of the IP areas (trademark, patent, or copyright) applicable to your venture?

Web Domains

Even if you aren't able to trademark a domain name, if you've built up a quality website with many inbound links, the website may have significant value to you. Be sure to keep a record showing when you need to renew your domain names. Sometimes, if a person becomes busy, he forgets to renew his domain name and somebody else purchases the domain with the intent to sell it back to the person.

The lesson is to realize what has value within your company and take basic precautions to protect it.

When forming a company website, many people create multiple domain names and point them to the same site. For example, thinkinglike.com and hupalo.com both point to the same content, my writing about entrepreneurship. I'd recommend against this, because your site's popularity will be a function of name recognition and also the number of inbound links to the site. It's usually better to have one domain name with 100 inbound links than two domains with 50 links each.

And, don't use a web domain which makes use of your service provider's domain. You want an independent name that could be moved to another Internet service provider (ISP) without losing previously established links.

Reputation

Reputation is an often overlooked aspect of proprietary products. A strong reputation helps encourage others to do business with your company. Because of this, it's important to build up your company's reputation. And, it's important to protect your company's reputation.

The value behind many companies is their reputation or brand identity. Consider companies such as: Charles Schwab in the stock brokerage business; Target or Best Buy in retailing; Amazon in book retailing; eBay in online auctions; or Mazda or BMW in car manufacture. People like to do business with these companies, because these companies have great reputations for outstanding service. These companies are the established leaders in their industry with huge name recognition.

While your home-based business probably doesn't aspire to have the national name recognition of an eBay or BMW, reputation is important. In fact, branding experts, such as Nick Wreden, author of *Fusion Branding: How To Forge Your Brand For The Future,* point out that product quality, great service, and reputation are crucial to establishing a positive brand identity.

The starting point for building a solid reputation is to deliver quality products and services. Every interaction a customer or potential customer has with your company makes an impression.

Harry Beckwith, author of *Selling The Invisible: A Field Guide To Modern Marketing,* and other business marketing experts suggest that you examine your company's "points of contact" with customers. Any interface between a customer or a potential customer and your company is a point of contact.

For example, if a customer calls you, the phone is a point of contact. How the phone is answered says something about your company. If the phone rings ten times before being answered, that will hurt a business's reputation. If a child picks up the phone, that hurts the business's reputation.

Examine all potential points of contact between your company and your customers and seek to improve the image made at each point of contact.

For people in the personal services area, such as consulting, reputation may be the most significant aspect of gaining profitable business.

Just as it's sometimes necessary to protect your company's IP rights, sometimes, you might need to legally protect your company's reputation. For example, there are some businesspeople who are active in combating consumer fraud. Business writers who expose scam artists and get-rich-quick gurus will sometimes find themselves attacked through anonymous posts on the Internet that maliciously make false and libelous statements.

Any false statement that harms the reputation of an individual is called defamation. Defamation is sometimes spoken (slander) or, today, more usually written (libel).

One effective way to combat personal attacks is to file what is known as a John Doe lawsuit against the anonymous poster. All posters to Internet websites leave behind information about the ISP they're using, called the IP address. That information can be used to track down the person to sue.

Filing a John Doe lawsuit will allow you to subpoena the Internet bulletin board and the ISP to obtain the true identity of the individual. A subpoena is a court order to the ISP to provide information the ISP has about the individual.

You may have read about John Doe lawsuits from the music industry. People suspected of sharing music illegally over the Internet had John Doe lawsuits filed against them for copyright infringement. It was a subpoena to the ISP that allowed these people to be identified.

Most of these people immediately settled the lawsuits, each paying the music companies several thousand dollars. While the music industry could have sought more (for example, their true legal fees), the purpose of the lawsuits was to force the people to pay just enough to make them realize they were violating the law, cease from downloading illegally, and notify other potential downloaders that there were consequences to violating copyright law. Another major goal was to make people on the Internet realize they aren't as anonymous as they think.

Fortunately, as a home-based business entrepreneur, you probably won't have hired and fired many employees, so disgruntled ex-employees won't pose a problem. However, be aware that if you're politically active, combat crime, or are involved in controversial causes, there is a possibility that someone who disagrees with your point of view will attack you maliciously over the Internet in an attempt to harm your business. You do have legal remedies at your disposal to deal with such individuals.

Some businesspeople would suggest avoiding controversial issues to minimize the likelihood of such attacks. For example, many marketing experts suggest participating in e-mail discussion groups or message boards to build traffic to your website. However, many times, online discussions go into political issues and other topics that are best avoided. And, many, ah, unique individuals hang out at message boards.

As a home business owner, you're almost certainly your company's best promotional tool. You're the ultimate point of contact between your business and the rest of the world. Consider the effects of everything you say and do and how it could affect your reputation.

Closely related to points of contact is the concept of gatekeepers. Gatekeepers are people who provide access to you or your business. While you'll usually want all the business referrals you can get, sometimes, in some businesses, it's necessary to screen out potential clients, customers, or associates. Gatekeepers serve this role.

For example, suppose you're a film producer or an angel investor. If you give everyone easy access to you, you'll be deluged with film scripts or business proposals. Dealing with so much "over the transom" material can prevent you from getting any real work done!

Larger companies often hire individuals to serve as gatekeepers. For example, most CEOs have personal assistants. As a solo, home-based entrepreneur, non-employees will need to serve this role of gatekeeper.

For example, if you're an angel investor, you may have several accountants and business lawyers who refer viable business plans to you. These people will know what kind of plans you want to see and what kind you don't.

Sometimes, there are other ways to screen out serious clients and customers from people who just want your time for free.

For example, many of the best attorneys don't offer free consultations. If you want to talk to them, you pay.

Some literary agents find themselves deluded with manuscripts from aspiring authors. Although I frown on the practice, because I think it opens the door to acting unethically, some agents have taken to charging "reading fees." They'll read your manuscript for $200 or so. Otherwise, they won't read a new writer's material at all.

While I can understand how this is used to help weed out less serious manuscripts, I dislike the fact that some "agents" earn several hundred thousand dollars per year just claiming to read hopeful authors' new books. Sometimes, these "agents" have little clout and few contacts, which makes their "agency" little better than a scam.

If you're a writer who contemplates paying a reading fee, always inquire about other books an agent has sold and how many of them were from first-time authors! Other agents have simply closed the doors to new over-the-transom manuscripts. To approach them, you'll need a reference.

As a new entrepreneur, you might find that networking with certain individuals would be desirable, either to obtain financing, establish a distribution or licensing deal, or pitch some idea.

Learning how to pass through gatekeepers can be a useful skill. Once you realize you must pass through a gatekeeper, ask yourself: What is this person looking for and how can I show them I have it? Who are the gatekeepers for the person I need to contact?

> Question: What are your company's points of contact? How can you improve them?
>
> Question: Are gatekeepers necessary to your type of business? If so, how will you build relationships with those positioned to send you profitable business?

The Value of Time

As a home-based entrepreneur, your time is important. Effective time management is crucial. It's easy to go out in the morning and play some tennis or golf. Then you come home and find some household chores that need doing. You do those. Then, you kick back for a hour or two to relax. Finally, your day is over, but you've achieved nothing for your business! At the end of some days, you might find yourself asking, "What exactly did I achieve today? Is it really possible to do so little in a day?!"

You must devote adequate time to your business for it to succeed. Failure to produce new products or market existing products can lead to a drop in revenue over time. Failure to devote time to current client projects can mean that you'll be in a serious time crunch if something unexpected comes up.

If you find you're not being productive, evaluate how you're spending your time. You might find you need to devote more time to your business. Sometimes, developing rituals will add structure to your day.

For example, if you're a writer, you might find that setting aside two hours each morning for writing works well for you. That time is devoted exclusively to writing. Once you sit down to write, you don't do anything else. Or, possibly, allowing two hours making sales calls in the morning is just what the business doctor ordered.

Studies have shown that people are more likely to continue exercise routines if they set aside a specific time of the day to exercise. Whatever your priorities are, consider structuring your day so that those priorities always have a time slot.

Try to follow the motto of Stephen Covey, author of *The Seven Habits of Highly Effective People*, who says that you should put first things first. In today's busy world, that's not always as easy as it sounds!

Just as it's easy to be diverted away from business by other interests or non-business duties, the reverse can also happen.

Because you don't work fixed hours away from home, it's easy to find yourself working many hours on your business at home. For the writer, it's easy to sit down at the computer and resume writing during the evening.

Be sure you don't burn yourself out by working too many hours, unless you really enjoy working those hours and the extra work hours aren't interfering with your family life. Allow some time for rejuvenation, rest, and non-business activities. Often, doing this will make you more creative and productive when you resume work.

Some entrepreneurs, who would otherwise tend to be workaholics, set a flat time limit on how much they'll work during the day. For example, five o'clock is quitting time, and no business-related work will be done after five o'clock.

It's interesting to note that if you work from home and don't travel as part of your business, you'll actually have more time. Many people spend an hour per day commuting. This time can be devoted to your business, family, or recreation.

Sometimes, it's valuable to monitor how you spend your business time and evaluate if you should be spending your time in different ways. Typically, time is spent in three different ways.

First, time is spent producing or developing products. For a computer programmer who works as a consultant, this time is spent writing computer code. For a builder of musical instruments, this time is spent building a violin.

Second, time is spent marketing products or services. This is typically time spent doing public relations or time spent contacting potential clients. It might be time on the phone or time spent writing a news release.

Third, time is spent doing the "overhead" duties of running a company. These are tasks that must be done, such as updating accounting records, doing taxes, or purchasing office supplies.

While time spent producing products or marketing products directly affects the bottom line, the administrative duties don't lead to new products being created or existing products being marketed. Administrative tasks don't directly lead to more profits. It's important to be careful that administrative tasks don't swamp the time you spend operating your business. Try to spend the bulk of your time either in creating products or marketing them.

Ultimately, time is your most proprietary product. It's yours. How you spend it is up to you. It's limited. It's the most valuable thing you possess.

Chapter 6
Limited Liability Companies
For Home Businesses

If you wish to gain the advantages of limited liability, but don't wish to incorporate, you can form a Limited Liability Company (LLC).

From a tax standpoint, LLCs are considered disregarded entities. This means if you form a one-person LLC, you continue to file your Schedule C with your personal 1040 tax return, just as if you operated as a sole proprietorship. From a federal tax-standpoint, your company is still considered a sole proprietorship.

LLC members who are active in running the business also continue to pay self-employment taxes, just as if you operated as a sole proprietorship. You aren't considered an "employee" of the LLC, with full employee tax reporting. And, you'd continue to make your personal estimated tax payments. The chapter about sole proprietor taxes (Schedule C, Schedule SE, and Form 1040-ES) fully applies to LLC owners.

If multiple people own the LLC, you'd file the partnership tax return Form 1065 for the LLC and each member active in running the company would pay self-employment taxes on his or her share of the earnings. Each individual would also continue to pay estimated taxes as an individual.

The main advantage of forming an LLC instead of a corporation is simplicity. Basically, you file some papers with your state, and your sole proprietorship becomes an LLC. Usually, such a filing is made with your secretary of state (or equivalent office). See the state-specific resources at the end of this book to learn more about filing to become an LLC in your state.

Here are some books for those who wish to read more about the LLC business structure: *Your Limited Liability Company: An Operating Manual* by Anthony Mancuso; *Form Your Own Limited Liability Company* by Anthony Mancuso and Beth Lawrence; and *Starting a Limited Liability Company* by Martin M. Shenkman.

S Corporations

Another attractive business structure for home-based businesses is the S corporation. The S corporation is similar to a regular corporation in most ways, except it's treated as a pass-through entity from a tax standpoint.

The advantage of an S corporation is that money not paid as wages is not subject to employment taxes. Money can be retained within the company or paid as dividends to minimize employment taxes. This often amounts to thousands of dollars per year in tax savings. Over a lifetime of earnings, those thousands of dollars, if invested and compounded in the stock market, can add up to millions of dollars.

Since many experts consider Social Security to be tenuous, some entrepreneurs might want to pay a reasonable, but minimal, salary from an S corporation and remove the rest of their company profits as S-corporation dividends.

Let's compare possible tax liabilities between an LLC and an S corporation. Assume your company earns $80,000 per year.

First, the LLC. As with a sole proprietorship, because you're an active member of running your LLC, your income is subject to Social Security taxes (i.e., self-employment taxes). This means you must pay Social Security self-employment tax on your net earnings up to the current wage base of $87,900 (as of 2004). The current rate is 15.3%, which includes both Social Security and Medicare contributions. Thus, you pay $12,240 in self-employment taxes. You pay this tax whether or not you plan to reinvest these net earnings in your company.

Second, the S corporation. Here you have some flexibility in the amount of salary you pay yourself. The IRS expects you to pay yourself a reasonable salary. Let's assume $40,000 per year is considered a reasonable salary. Money that remains in the company or is distributed as S-corporation dividends isn't subject to employment taxes. Thus, you pay only $6,120 in employment taxes.

Comparing the employment taxes, we see the S corporation allows us to save $6,120 per year over the LLC.

However, an S corporation is more complex than an LLC in that officers of the corporation are treated as employees. This means the corporation is subject to full employee wage reporting, even if there is only a single owner-employee. The corporation also needs to file its own tax return, Form 1120S (and shareholders of the corporation need to be given K-1 forms annually). You will no longer file Schedule C along with your personal tax return. And, certain corporate formalities, such as holding stockholder meetings and documenting key corporate decisions with resolutions, are also required.

If you have relatively high company earnings ($80,000 and up) for your home-based business and you wish to reduce Social Security taxes, I'd consider forming an S corporation. Otherwise, forming an LLC is an excellent option relative to operating a sole proprietorship.

I discuss S corporations in more detail in my book *How To Start And Run Your Own Corporation: S-Corporations For Small Business Owners*. New corporation owners might also want to acquire a copy of *The Corporate Minutes Book: The Legal Guide to Taking Care of Corporate Business* by Anthony Mancuso to help them understand corporate formalities.

Chapter 7
Business Expenses

What are considered legitimate business expenses for a home-based business? Typically, any expense that is considered ordinary or necessary to operate your company qualifies as a business expense. (See IRS Publication 535: *Business Expenses* for more information.)

If the significant benefit of incurring the expense goes to benefit the owners of the business, rather than being necessary or useful to the business, itself, you'll need to see if any special rules apply to limit or disallow the tax-deductibility of the expense.

Business owners generally like to seek out legitimate, tax-deductible business expenses, because it's the net income of the business that's usually subject to income tax.

Sales Revenue - Expenses = Net Income

Let's examine some legitimate business expenses. Suppose you operate a newsletter publishing business. You do a direct mail marketing promotion that costs $10,000 and generates 200 subscribers to your newsletter.

The $10,000 is considered a marketing or advertising expense. It's ordinary to the newsletter publishing business and is fully deductible. Of course, the $10,000 spent to attract new customers obviously isn't "necessary," but it's still tax deductible, because the expense is useful to the business in increasing revenue and profits.

Over the course of the year, suppose you send out your monthly newsletter to these 200 subscribers, printing a total of 2,400 newsletters. The printing cost of these newsletters is $500. Suppose mailing these newsletters costs $1,000. Clearly, the printing costs and the mailing costs are necessary to your business. These are also legitimate, tax-deductible expenses.

Assume your newsletter is priced at $200, so that your company revenue is $40,000. So far, your taxable income looks like:

Revenue - Expenses = Net Income

```
   $40,000
 -  10,000
 -     500
 -   1,000
   _____

   $28,500
```

We see the net taxable income is $28,500. Of course, other expenses might be incurred. For example, you might hire freelance writers to contribute articles or analysis to your newsletter. If you paid a writer $200 for an article, this $200 becomes a tax-deductible expense.

A question arises. What if you pay *yourself* $200 for an article *you* contribute to your newsletter? Is this a legitimate business expense? Clearly, the benefit of the $200 goes to you.

If you did wish to pay yourself $200 for your writing contribution, this payment would only be legally tax deductible if you also reported the $200 as personal income somewhere else. Schedule C would be the most appropriate place to report this income (self-employed writers typically use Schedule C). Thus, your income and expenses would *both* increase by $200, which wouldn't be useful. (We're assuming you operate as a sole proprietorship and report all expenses and earnings with one Schedule C).

Typically, as a sole proprietor, you would not pay yourself for the article. Rather, part of your regular duties of operating the newsletter would include writing. Then, the net profits of the enterprise would go to you, and you could spend them as you wished. *We see that sole proprietors shouldn't consider their time or payments to themselves as expenses.*

Payments to non-related parties for work performed are tax-deductible expenses. Of course, because you and your sole proprietorship are considered the same, you could pay yourself $200 if you wished. It's just that it wouldn't be reported as a business expense. Instead, you'd just be withdrawing some of the profits from the company.

Suppose after printing the newsletters, you packed them into your new SUV and drove the newsletters to the post office for mailing. Driving the newsletters to the post office is necessary. Does this mean the full purchase price of the SUV is a legitimate business expense?

Clearly, you use the SUV for many other personal purposes, such as picking the kids up after school, going skiing, or carrying groceries. Because the business use is relatively trivial, it wouldn't be proper to claim a deduction for the SUV. (See IRS Publication 463: *Travel, Entertainment, Gift And Car Expenses* for more information about the deductibility of car and travel expenses. The IRS distinguishes between cars and SUVs).

Technically, you're entitled to a tax deduction for that portion of the time you use the vehicle for your business, but because that time is so small relative to the overall use, it probably isn't worth bothering with. It might not be worth the tax deduction to spend the time recording the business and non-business use of the SUV.

However, if you operated an electrical contracting company which involved driving around the neighborhood to jobs and the SUV were used exclusively for business purposes, then the full cost of the SUV would be a proper business expense. Currently, you'd be able to expense (deduct) the full cost of the SUV in the year the vehicle was purchased and placed into service.

Even if you used the SUV for some personal use, the IRS might accept your deduction for the full amount. In any case, most of the cost of the SUV would be deductible.

The SUV is considered a long-lived asset in that the asset generates value over many years. Such long-lived assets are usually *depreciated*, which means that their expense (and tax deduction) is spread over several years. You only get to deduct a portion of the cost of the asset each year, until the asset is fully deducted. However, many long-lived assets used by home business owners qualify for Section 179 expense deduction, which allows the full cost of a long-lived asset to be written off in the year the asset is placed in service.

Some long-lived assets that can be deducted in one year include:

• Off-The-Shelf Software
• Tangible Personal Property, Such As Machinery

If your income is high, it's usually good to use Section 179 and deduct the cost of long-lived assets immediately, if allowed. This maximizes your current tax benefit. However, if your income is lower, sometimes it's beneficial to use depreciation, which allows you to use the expense against future years, when you might be in a higher tax bracket.

IRS Publication 946: *Depreciation* covers depreciation and Section 179 expenses in more detail.

We see a legitimate expense to one business might not be a legitimate expense to another business. The SUV was a legitimate expense to the electrical contractor, but not to the newsletter publisher.

Similarly, this is the reason behind the IRS hobby loss rule. The idea is that hobbies and the equipment to enjoy them aren't tax deductible. The only hobby that's tax deductible is making money!

So, if you're a tennis professional who actually earns money playing tennis, then the cost of your tennis rackets, tennis balls, and tennis racket restringing are all tax deductible. But, if you only play tennis as a hobby, these costs aren't tax deductible.

If you're a professional photographer, the costs of your cameras, lights, and tripods are tax deductible. If photography is only a hobby to you and you don't earn money doing it, then these costs aren't tax deductible.

The IRS typically expects to see home-based businesses earning a profit within the first three years. If your business is particularly "fun," involves expensive equipment that is also used for hobbies, and you fail to earn profits over several years, the IRS might deem your business to be a hobby and disallow future tax deductions for it. You can, of course, always appeal to show that you really are trying to make money. And, if you earn money in the future, the expenses will become deductible. See IRS Publication 535: *Business Expenses* for more detail about exactly what constitutes a hobby.

Many home-based businesses won't need to worry about the hobby loss rule, because the business will be profitable relatively soon after it's started. Home-based businesses tend to have low investments in capital assets, low overhead, and low expenses which are directly tied to the level of business activity. This usually leads to profitability.

Tax Deductibility of Health Insurance

Because the government wants to encourage people to have health insurance, recently, health insurance has become a tax-deductible expense to all business owners who pay for their own health insurance. This is true whether the company is operated as a corporation, an LLC, or a sole proprietorship (Schedule C business). This deduction appears on Line 31 of the 1040 tax return (see the sample 1040 tax return in the chapter about taxes). If you pay for your own health insurance, be sure you take advantage of this deduction.

Amortizing Business Start-Up Costs

Suppose you invest money to prepare to start a business. For example, you purchase books about the business or you travel to meet distributors or customers. These expenses could be incurred years before you actually start your business, but they are ultimately related to starting your business. When your business actively begins, these costs become tax deductible.

Typically, these start-up costs are amortized (spread) over five years, and you deduct 20% of the total cost each year for five years. For example, if your total start-up costs are $1,000, you'd deduct $200 per year for your first five years of business operation. See IRS Publication: 535 *Business Expenses* for more detail. Be sure to keep receipts of your start-up expenses as you research your business endeavor and amortize these expenses incurred in years before you start operations.

Research and experimental costs are amortized over ten years. These costs apply to research which typically leads to patents. So, if you're an inventor who has incurred considerable costs to develop an idea, those costs are amortized over ten years. Most home-based businesses will only have start-up costs amortized over five years.

Amortization and depreciation are very similar in that each year a portion of an expense is deducted until the expense is fully deducted.

Keeping Receipts

Sole proprietorships are one of the business structures most heavily audited by the IRS, although your actual chance of being audited is very slight. You're expected to keep documentation of all of your business expenses. Keep your receipts for business purchases.

Why are modest sole proprietorships more heavily audited than S corporations and other more advanced business structures? Partly, it's because sole proprietors tend to do their own taxes and make more mistakes. Partly, it's a sad result of political factors. As David Cay Johnson, author of *Perfectly Legal: The Covert Campaign To Rig Our Tax System To Benefit The Super Rich—And Cheat Everybody Else*, explains, the IRS has been remade so that it seldom properly punishes the super rich who fail to pay their taxes, while spending more time pursuing middle-class and poorer people. This isn't the fault of the IRS. It's the result of the pressures put on the IRS by political forces.

So, if you purchase some pens, stationery, and envelopes from Quill.com, keep the receipt showing the purchase. These receipts can be stored in a manilla envelope. It's also good to record the year on the envelope, so all your 2005 receipts will be together, all your 2006 receipts will be together, etc. Although you'll probably never need to look at these receipts again, it's important to have them, if you're ever audited.

A good book to help you understand how to avoid IRS audits is *Minding Her Own Business: The Self-Employed Woman's*

Guide To Taxes and Recordkeeping by IRS enrolled agent Jan Zobel.

Sometimes, it might not be immediately clear why a particular cost is a legitimate business expense. When a question might arise, it's good to record exactly why a particular expense is a legitimate business expense.

For example, my small book publishing company produced a photographically-intense book about how to build a PC. To do this, some photography equipment was purchased. When the equipment was purchased, that the equipment was for this book's production was written down. Similarly, a copy of Linux, the operating system, was purchased. Screen captures were used to demonstrate installing Linux on a new PC in the book. Two or three years down the road, without recording the purpose of some of this stuff, it might be difficult to remember exactly why this stuff was purchased and how it related to the business at the time. What might seem obvious to you now might become mysterious in the future, so making notes is handy!

Of course, the purpose of most purchases is obvious and needs no special notations. For example, if padded mailing envelopes are purchased, it's obviously for packing things to mail.

Photography equipment is classified as listed property by the IRS. (IRS Publication 946: *Depreciation* discusses listed property in more detail.) Listed property is property that is typically used for entertainment, recreation, or amusement. Listed property includes passenger vehicles with a weight less than 6,000 pounds and computers. SUVs aren't considered listed property. That's because they tend to be classified as working trucks.

Special rules apply to listed property, because listed property is considered stuff people might like to purchase for their own personal use, but claim a tax deduction for business use. It's usually expected that records will be kept of how listed property is used.

To be deductible as a Section 179 expense, for example, it's required that the listed property be used for business at least 50% of the time. Recording the business use of the property helps establish its deductibility, if it's ever questioned.

Documenting Other Sources of Non-Business Revenue

While the IRS is alert to people seeking improper expenses to inappropriately reduce taxable income, they're also alert that some nefarious business owners underreport their income. Because of this, it's important to document sources of non-business income you receive. For example, if your brother-in-law repays a $10,000 loan to you, it's good to make a note of the source of the $10,000. That way, if you're ever audited, you'll be able to quickly explain the source of the income and that it isn't revenue from your business and that it isn't taxable.

Depreciation Worksheets

Depreciation, Section 179 expense deductions, and listed property are all reported on IRS form 4562, which attaches to your business tax return.

For any long-term assets that you depreciate, you'll want to keep a depreciation worksheet. (IRS Publication 946 has a sample). Record the date the item was placed in service, its cost, and the annual depreciation. Record the depreciation deduction previously taken in past years. This allows you to quickly see how much of the asset has already been depreciated and how much remains to be depreciated. Having this worksheet will make doing your taxes in future years easier.

For example, before off-the-shelf software became deductible under Section 179 (where it's expensed in the year purchased), it previously needed to be depreciated over five years.

Thus, if you were a small publisher and you purchased the page layout program Pagemaker for $500, you had to depreciate it over five years. Suppose you used straight-line depreciation where equal amounts are depreciated each year. You had to deduct $100 per year for each of five years.

Suppose you purchased the software at the end of 2002. In 2003, you deducted $100. In 2004, you deducted $100. In 2005, $300 remain to be deducted, and you'll deduct $100 in 2005. Without a depreciation worksheet, you'll probably forget what to do in 2006, and you'll get frustrated with the time you're spending doing your taxes! Or you'll forget that you still have a deduction coming for the purchase of Pagemaker!

For one purchase, it seems easy enough to remember. But, if you also purchased Photoshop in 2003, MYOB in 2001, etc., you'll really be glad you kept a depreciation worksheet when you figure your taxes!

Of course, this can be even more complicated because first year depreciation might not allow all of the $100! Instead, for the first year, you might only be allowed to depreciate an amount proportional to the amount of time the item was in service. If it was used for half the year, you'll only be able to deduct $50 in the first year. If it was used for one month, you'll depreciate $8.33 the first year, with the rest depreciated in future years.

Many small business owners jumped up and down with glee when off-the-shelf software became deductible under Section 179, so the full cost could be expensed in the year the software was purchased. It's not so much getting a bigger tax break that made them happy, but rather being able to do away with recording depreciation.

It's possible as a home-based business owner that you'll have no depreciable assets. All of your long-term assets might be able to be written off (expensed, depreciated) in the year the item is purchased. If so, you won't need to bother keeping a depreciation worksheet.

Cash-Based Accounting Versus Accrual-Based Accounting

The IRS requires most businesses which carry inventory to use accrual-based accounting. Many home businesses without inventory operate on cash-based accounting. Some people argue that cash-based accounting is better and easier. But, I believe, once you're familiar with whichever accounting convention you use, cash or accrual, you'll have an easy time.

Accrual-based accounting and cash-based accounting have different ways of recognizing when revenue and expenses are recorded. See IRS Publication 538: *Accounting Periods and Methods* for more detail about the difference between accrual-based and cash-based accounting.

For example, consider your business checkbook. Every time you write a check, you see an expense is incurred. Writing the check corresponds to a cash outflow (assuming the check is cashed, of course!). So if you purchase ten reams of copy paper for $20 and your checkbook balance was $300, your new balance is $280. When entering your checks in Quicken, for example, you'd add $20 to office supply expense. When the cash left your company, it became an expense. So if you wrote the check on October 18, 2004, you'd record the expense as occurring on October 18, 2004. That's how cash-based accounting works with expenses.

However, suppose you purchased the same ten reams of copy paper on account. You've created a liability for $20. With cash-based accounting, you wouldn't recognize this expense until you received an invoice and paid the invoice. However, with accrual-based accounting, you'd recognize the expense as soon as you incurred *the obligation* to pay for the copy paper. This would correspond to placing your order.

Example: You purchase ten reams of copy paper on December 29, 2004, on account for $20. The paper is received January 2, 2005. The invoice is received on January 15, 2005. Under cash-based accounting, you'd record the expense on the date you paid the invoice—January 15, 2005, for example. This expense occurs in the 2005 tax year.

Under accrual-based accounting, this $20 expense applies to the 2004 tax year, because you have incurred the obligation for the expense in 2004.

Notice the advantage of accrual-based accounting as it relates to expenses. Toward the year's end, you can increase your tax-deductible expenses by making legitimate business purchases. Even though no cash flows out to pay for those expenses before the year's end, the expense becomes tax deductible in the current year.

Revenue recognition also works differently under the two types of accounting. Cash-based accounting recognizes revenue when cash is *received* from the customer. Accrual-based accounting recognizes the sale when *the obligation to pay* is incurred by the customer.

Suppose you sell a custom closet design to a customer on account for $200 and you invoice the customer on December 29, 2004. The customer pays you on January 10, 2005.

Question: Under cash-based accounting, when is the sale recorded? When is the sale taxable as income to your business? Under accrual-based accounting, when is the sale recorded as occurring, and when does the income from the sale become taxable to your business? Write your answers down before continuing!

Answer: Under cash-based accounting, the sale is recognized when the cash for the sale is received—January 10, 2005. That's also when the income is reported. So, the $200 in income becomes taxable in 2005. Under accrual-based accounting, the customer's obligation to pay occurred on December 29, 2004. Thus, the $200 sales revenue is recognized on December 29, 2004, and this sales revenue becomes taxable in 2004, even though payment for the sale isn't received until 2005.

We see the disadvantage to recording sales on accrual-based accounting. You might wind up owing income tax for a sale that won't be paid for until next year! That might mean you have to come up with cash to pay this tax without having cash from the sale. This is one reason many entrepreneurs prefer cash-based accounting.

For example, Dan Poynter, author of *The Self-Publishing Manual*, favors cash-based accounting. Book publishers who have inventory must record inventory on an accrual-based accounting basis. Mixing cash-based accounting for non-inventory items and using accrual for inventory is called hybrid accounting, part accrual, part cash.

While cash-based accounting has some advantages, it's generally agreed that accrual-based accounting provides a more accurate reflection of how your business is doing.

New home business entrepreneurs can usually use either accounting method. If the IRS allows you to use cash-based accounting, if you have large revenue sales per customer, and if you sell to customers where payment might be received much later than the sale is generated, you might want to choose cash-based accounting.

On the other hand, if you have credit policies which pretty much guarantee cash is received with the sale and if defaults or non-payments are rare, then you might want to use accrual accounting.

Credit Policies And Accounts Receivable

In *Thinking Like An Entrepreneur: How To Make Intelligent Business Decisions That Will Lead To Success In Building And Growing Your Own Company*, I discuss establishing credit policies and how companies in competitive industries often must provide lax payment options, such as no-money down, no-money due for one year. I explain how this is a fundamental weakness in a business model.

The typical home business entrepreneur can't afford to offer excessively generous credit policies. Nonpayments can seriously cut into a small business's profitability, because with each nonpayment, you're not only out the profit you would have made on the sale, but you're out the cost of the goods sold, plus any other costs to generate and fill the order.

The trend is to collect payment with the order if you sell relatively low-priced products (for example, under $200). For example, payment by cash, check, or money order would be accepted. If customers wanted to purchase the item on credit, you'd usually accept credit cards, but wouldn't offer credit directly.

On the other hand, in many businesses, offering credit is standard policy. You'll lose sales if you don't offer customers the opportunity to order now, but pay later. Many businesses which serve other businesses fall into this category.

Monitoring your accounts receivable is crucial. You don't want to continue to extend credit to non-paying customers. Accounts receivable refers to the money owed your company by your customers. Accounts payable is the money your company owes other companies.

If you have a software accounting program, be sure to generate a report showing how much each customer owes you. An aging schedule will show if customers are behind on their payments. Some businesses have failed because they didn't monitor accounts receivable. What was carried on the books as a large asset, accounts receivable, turned out to be relatively worthless.

Use Tax

Many business owners will purchase supplies online from companies located outside of their state. For these sales, state sales tax hasn't been collected. Many states expect you to collect and pay your own sales tax for these sales. When you collect and pay your own sales tax, it's called *use tax*.

For example, in Minnesota, a state sales tax of 6.5% applies to all retail sales. If a business owner purchased a computer online for $1,000 and no sales tax was collected, the state would expect you to fork over $65 for sales tax. You would pay $65 in use tax.

Find out what rules your state has regarding use tax. Not paying use tax is one of the most common problems that could turn up if the state audited your books. For example, if you've claimed tax-deductible purchases and show an online store receipt that doesn't show sales tax, the auditor could quickly learn if you've paid use tax for the out-of-state purchase.

For more information about business expenses and/or accounting, I recommend these books: *Keeping the Books: Basic Record Keeping and Accounting for the Successful Small Business* by Linda Pinson; *422 Tax Deductions for Businesses and Self-Employed Individuals* by Bernard Kamoroff; and *Minding Her Own Business: The Self-Employed Woman's Guide To Taxes and Recordkeeping* by Jan Zobel.

Chapter 8
Home-Based Business Taxes

This chapter will introduce you to the three IRS tax forms you'll most likely need as a home-based entrepreneur who operates as a sole proprietor or as a limited liability company (LLC). Those forms are:

1) Schedule C (or C-EZ) for reporting your self-employment income from your sole proprietorship. Schedule C is attached to your personal 1040 income tax return. Schedule C also applies to one-member limited liability companies (LLCs).

2) Schedule SE which reports your self-employment tax (SE tax). As a sole proprietor, you pay into the Social Security system and Medicare on your net earnings from self-employment. Schedule SE is attached to your personal IRS 1040 income tax return. Schedule SE also applies to one-member limited liability companies where the member is active in running the business.

3) Form 1040-ES and estimated tax payments. If you anticipate having taxable earnings from which income tax isn't withheld, estimated tax payments are required four times a year. Estimated tax payments apply to all business owners who expect to owe income tax beyond their other tax withholdings.

If you operate your home-based business as an S corporation, my book *How To Start And Run Your Own Corporation: S-Corporations For Small Business Owners* covers S-corporation taxes in detail, including completed tax returns.

Before reading this chapter, you might want to go to IRS.gov and click on "Forms and Publications" and then go to "Forms and Instructions" and download the following forms: 1040 (f1040.pdf); Schedule C for the 1040 (f1040sc.pdf); Schedule SE (f1040sse.pdf); and Schedule ES (f1040es.pdf). Then, print out the forms to help you follow along.

I also suggest getting a copy of IRS Publication 334: *Tax Guide For Small Business*. If you don't like reading booklets online, the IRS can provide a paper version (IRS phone: 1-800-829-3676). That booklet does a good job of explaining the tax issues sole proprietors face.

Janet's Advertising Design

For our example, we'll assume Janet operates a desktop publishing business. (Janet's tax forms are included at the end of this chapter.) She charges clients $75 per hour to create print brochures and other advertising material. Janet also self-publishes a book called *Janet On Advertising*. We'll have her write a book so that we can demonstrate cost of goods sold (cogs). A pure service business probably wouldn't have a cost of goods sold.

During the year, Janet generates 500 billable hours for a total service revenue of $37,500. She also prints 1,000 copies of her new book *Janet On Advertising* at a cost of $3,000. Shipping charges for her to receive the books are $200.

She charges $15 for her book and sells it from her website. But, she only sells 100 copies during her first year for a total revenue from book sales of $1,500. The cost of goods sold is 100 copies times $3, the cost per copy, or $300.

Janet purchases a color printer for $400; an ergonomic chair for $200; and a computer system for $1,000. These expenses represent her fixed (or long-lived) assets. She also spends $500 for paper; $400 for postage; and $500 for business phone expense. She subscribes to a magazine called *Desktop Publishing Today* for $20 per year to help her stay current in her field.

Janet's income statement looks like this:

Revenue:

$37,500	Service Revenue
$1,500	Book Sales Revenue
$39,000	Total Gross Receipts

Depreciable Expenses For Long-Lived Assets:

$400	Color Printer
$200	Ergonomic Chair
$1,000	Computer System
$1,600	Total Depreciable Assets

Janet will elect to expense these depreciable assets in the current year using Section 179 expense deduction. (IRS Form 4562: *Depreciation and Amortization* would be attached to her Schedule C. Form 4562 reports Section 179 expense deduction.) Thus, the total Section 179 expense that Janet will claim is $1,600.

Current Year Expenses:

$300	Cost of Goods Sold For Physical Products (cogs is usually closely tied to product sales revenue and is usually separated from other current expenses.)
$200	Shipping/Freight Expense For Books Received
$500	Paper
$400	Postage
$500	Business Phone Expense
$20	*Desktop Publishing Today* subscription

$1,920

Net Profit from operating her business:

Revenue - Expenses = Net Income

Total Gross Receipts	$39,000
Less Current Year Expenses	$1,920
Less Section 179 Deductions	$1,600
Net Income (Profit)	$35,480

More conventionally, cogs is listed immediately after sales revenue and separated from other currrent year expenses:

Total Gross Receipts	$39,000
Less COGS	-$300
Gross Profit	$38,700
Less Current Year Expenses	-$1,620
Less Section 179 Deductions	-$1,600
Net Income (Profit)	$35,480

Although Janet works out of her home, she hasn't set aside a particular room or area to operate her business, so she doesn't qualify for or claim a deduction for the use of her home office. She doesn't have any employees and doesn't have an Employer Identification Number (EIN).

Schedule C

Schedule C is an IRS schedule attached to your 1040 income tax return that reports your income or loss from running a sole proprietorship. You only file Schedule C at the end of the year with your 1040 tax return. We show Janet's Schedule C at the end of this chapter. As you read this section, you might want to keep flipping back to the Schedule C when specific lines are mentioned. Or, print out the forms from IRS.gov and follow along on those forms.

Notice the lines of interest. On Line F, we select our accounting method—cash, accrual, or other. Cash versus accrual accounting is described in another chapter. Many service businesses prefer cash-based accounting. Companies which require inventory will need to use accrual for their sales and inventory.

If Janet had only operated as a desktop publisher (a service business) and didn't have inventory, she might prefer cash accounting. But, with inventory, she'll need to select either accrual or specify "Other." In describing "Other," she could say her inventory and product sales of inventory were on accrual. But, everything else was on a cash basis. We'll select "Accrual" for Janet's desktop publishing business. "Other" would also be a good choice, because the bulk of her revenue is service generated.

In Part I, Income, Line 1 asks for gross receipts or sales, also known as revenue. Janet had $39,000 in revenue. Line 2 allows for returns. Janet feels her customers won't return her products, so she doesn't enter any value for returns.

To determine Line 4, Cost of Goods Sold (cogs), we need to go to Page 2, Part III of Schedule C. Most inventory is valued at cost. To calculate cogs, typically, the inventory at the start of the year is added to any purchases of inventory made during the year. This total is the total inventory available for selling throughout the year. From this total value of inventory available for selling, the remaining value of inventory at year end is subtracted. The final result, cogs, is the value of the inventory sold during the year.

Inventory at start of year + Purchases of inventory during the year - Inventory at end of year = cogs

During the year, Janet purchased $3,000 worth of books to sell (Line 36). She purchased 1,000 books for $3,000. Her inventory at the start of the year was zero (Line 35). Because her cost per book was $3 and 900 books remain at the end of the year, the inventory at the end of the year is $2,700. Thus, her cogs (Line 42) is $3,000 minus $2,700 or $300. That number exactly corresponds to the inventory cost of the books sold—100 books times $3 per book.

Suppose Janet only counted 890 books. Then her ending inventory would have been $2,670. Her cost of goods sold would have been $3,000 minus $2,670 or $330. That corresponds to 110 books. The extra ten books missing might have been due to theft or damage. If you notice your year end inventory seems low, examine the cause. Products given away for marketing purposes are also often figured into cogs, but it's good to know exactly where your inventory is going.

Line 42 is $300 and this also becomes Line 4 on Page 1 (cogs). To get Line 5, Gross Profit, we subtract cogs ($300) from sales ($39,000) to get $38,700. Thus, Line 7, Gross Income, is $38,700.

From Janet's gross income, she will subtract her business expenses to determine her taxable income. Part II of Schedule

C is used to calculate your expenses. The key point here is that an expense must only be recorded in one place!

For example, if you spend $1,000 to hire a publicist, that value could be reported on Line 8, Advertising Expense. However, if you weren't sure it was Advertising Expense, you could report it on Line 27, Other Expenses, and explain what the expense was.

"Other expenses" is particularly valuable for reporting expenses if you're not sure where else they should go. Part V of Schedule C shows space for describing your "Other Expenses." You can also attach a sheet of paper to give you more room. If your expenses are fully legitimate, the conventional wisdom is that the more detail you provide, the less likely you are to be audited. When the IRS isn't sure what the expense actually is, it's more likely to doubt its legitimacy.

A few lines are of particular interest. Line 13 describes Depreciation and Section 179 expense. This will correspond to the color printer, ergonomic chair, and computer system which total $1,600.

Line 15 is for business insurance. Health insurance isn't entered here. Rather, your health insurance deduction is entered directly on Page 1 of your 1040 tax form (Line 31 of 1040).

Line 19 is for tax deductible pension plans. Those aren't to be confused with your own self-employment SEP or SIMPLE IRA which is reported on Page 1 (Line 32) of the 1040.

Line 24 is for travel and entertainment expenses. Be sure to keep receipts for these. Also be sure you can explain why the expense is a legitimate business expense. Was it dinner with a client or a business trip to Hawaii? Which client? What business was done in Hawaii?

Line 26 is for wages paid to others. Not money Janet pays herself. Any net earnings from a sole proprietorship belong to the sole proprietor and he/she can remove the earnings at will. The IRS only cares about your reporting your net self-employment income, not about how much money you're taking out of your sole proprietorship

Line 27, Other Expenses, is $1,620. Notice cogs isn't included here. It's included in Part I.

Line 28 is Janet's total expense for operating her business. Adding Line 8 to Line 27, we get a total expense value of $3,220. A quick subtraction of Janet's total expenses (Line 28) from Janet's gross income (Line 7) shows she's earned $35,480 as her taxable income from business operations (Line 29), without allowing for a home office deduction.

If you choose to deduct expenses for the business use of your home, enter this on Line 30 and attach IRS Form 8829.

We see that Janet has a net profit of $35,480 as entered on Line 31. The instructions for Line 31 are clear. They say we must enter net profit on Line 12 of our 1040 tax return and also on Schedule SE, Line 2, to help us calculate our self-employment tax.

If you look at Janet's 1040, you'll see she entered $35,480 on Line 12, "Business Income (or loss). Attach schedule C or C-EZ." Don't forget to attach Schedule C to your 1040 when filing your taxes.

You now understand the basics of Schedule C. Essentially all Schedule C does is to take your income and subtract your expenses from your income to determine your taxable business income.

Schedule SE (Self-Employment Tax)

Now that we've been told to enter $35,480 on Line 2 of Schedule SE, we'll move on to Schedule SE, which is used to calculate the taxes you'll owe Social Security and Medicare.

Line 3 says, "Combine lines 1 and 2," which means add them. So, Line 3 is $35,480.

Line 4 says to "Multiply line 3 by 92.35% (.9235)" to determine your "Net earnings from Self-Employment." This line basically says you don't owe self-employment tax on all of your earnings, but only on 92.35% of your earnings. Multiplying $35,480 by 0.9235, we get $32,765.78 for Line 4.

So, what's up with this line? Why multiply by 92.35%? That's lobbying from the calculator industry. (Just kidding. But, you'll definitely want to buy a simple calculator when you start your business. You can get a decent one, such as a Texas Instruments TI35, for $10.)

The IRS decided you shouldn't owe self-employment tax on *all* the money you pay into self-employment tax. Thus, you get to reduce your net self-employment earnings by one-half of the amount you pay into self-employment tax. Self-employment tax is at the rate of 15.3% (of this 12.4% is Social Security and 2.9% is Medicare). So you're taxed on $(1- 0.153/2) = 0.9235$ of your income.

Whenever you see tax deductions that allow for one-half of your self-employment tax, this is an attempt to make sole proprietor self-employment taxes more comparable to employment taxes. Employers typically pay one-half of an employee's Social Security and Medicare tax. This payment is tax deductible to employers. And, employees aren't forced to pay Social Security tax on this extra little amount. (I still suspect the calculator people had a hand in it.)

Line 5 calculates your self-employment tax as 15.3% of Line 4. Here, Janet owes $32,765.78 times 15.3% or $5,013.16 in SE taxes. The instructions say to also enter the Line 5 amount on Line 57 of your 1040. Line 57 of your 1040 lists other taxes you owe in addition to income tax. Self-employment tax is listed here. Janet must pay an extra $5,013.16 to Uncle Sam.

This applies for self-employment income which is less than $87,900. $87,900 is called the Social Security wage base (2004). Only wages up to this wage base are subject to Social Security taxes. So, CEOs who earn $10 million per year in compensation don't need to pay Social Security tax on the amount above $87,900. However, Medicare has no wage base. Thus, those CEOs must pay 2.9% Medicare tax on all their earnings.

Incidentally, forming an S corporation is one way to reduce employment taxes, because S-corporation dividends avoid employment tax. During the 2004 Presidential Election, it was pointed out that Senator John Edwards saved $591,000 in Medicare taxes by forming his own S corporation. When you earn tens of millions of dollars, even 2.9% really adds up! For more information about how S corporations can reduce your self-employment taxes, see my book *How To Start And Run Your Own Corporation: S-Corporations For Small Business Owners.*

Line 6 calculates one-half of your self-employment tax. One half of Line 5 ($5,013.16) is $2,506.58. The instructions say to enter this on Line 30 of your 1040. This will *reduce* Janet's taxable income by $2,506.58. You're allowed to deduct one-half of what you pay into Social Security and Medicare from your income taxes.

You now understand the basics of Self-Employment taxes and Schedule SE.

With Schedule C and Schedule SE completed, we can fill out the rest of Janet's 1040 tax return. Line 12 of the 1040 is "Business income or (loss). Attach Schedule C or C-EZ." This is where Janet entered $35,480.00. (Notice, if Janet had operated as an S-corporation, her S-corporation pass through income would be listed on Line 17, not Line 12.)

We assume Janet had no other income, so Line 22, Janet's total income, is $35,480.00. Moving on to the section "Adjusted Gross Income," we see several lines of interest to business owners.

Line 30 is "One-half of self-employment tax. Attach Schedule SE." That amount is $2,506.58. This will reduce Janet's tax income by $2,506.58. Don't forget to attach Schedule SE to your personal 1040 tax return when you file it.

Line 31 is "Self-employed health insurance deduction." Janet doesn't have health insurance in our example. But, if she paid her own health insurance, this is where her total health insurance premiums would be listed. So, if Janet paid $300 per month in health insurance, she'd list $3,600 here, which would reduce her taxable income by $3,600.

Line 32 is for "Self-employed SEP, SIMPLE, and qualified [retirement] plans." When your business has more income, forming your own SEP is one way to shelter more of your income from taxation. See a brokerage firm, such as Vanguard, for more information about forming an SEP or other self-employed retirement account. These accounts are basically like one-person 401(k)s. You can invest in any mutual funds, stocks, bonds, money market funds, or CDs. Notice that regular IRA deductions are reported on Line 25.

We see Janet has an adjusted gross income of $32,973.42. Moving on to Page 2 of Janet's 1040, Janet uses the standard deduction. She's also single. (Sorry guys. She's dating somebody!)

Line 42 shows Janet's taxable income is $25,023.42. And, the tax tables show she owes $3,396.00 in income tax. Janet pays about 14% of her AGI in income tax.

Notice that Janet is in for a surprise under "Other Taxes." Line 57 is "Self-employment tax. Attach Schedule SE." Janet's self-employment tax is $5,013.16. Adding Janet's income tax to her self-employment tax shows she owes a total of $8,409.16. She'll need to check to see if she owes a penalty on Line 75.

Janet's tax bill was so large because there were no tax withholdings from her income. When you have earnings that aren't subject to wage withholding, you usually do your own version of "withholding," called estimated tax payments.

Estimated Tax Payments

Notice that Janet owes the IRS an extra $5,013.16 in self-employment taxes in 2004. Plus, she owes income tax on her self-employment earnings of $3,396.00. The U.S. income tax system is a pay-as-you-go system. As you earn money, the IRS wants its share. For individuals with significant income that isn't subject to withholding, the IRS expects estimated tax payments.

As a business owner, it's good to estimate your income and make the appropriate estimated tax payments. You generally must pay 90% of your estimated income tax to avoid a penalty. However, if you pay an amount equal to your last year's tax (110% if your AGI is over $150,000), you also avoid a penalty.

Estimated tax payments are due in four installments. Typically, the due dates are April 15, June 15, September 15, and January 15. When you receive your 1040-ES payment vouchers, they'll include the date each tax payment is due.

Let's assume Janet is planning for 2004, *which will now be treated as the upcoming year.* (As this book is being written, 2005 1040-ES forms weren't available yet. If you were planning *for 2005, you'd use 2005 1040-ES forms.* You can always get the most current IRS forms available by visiting IRS.gov and going to "Forms and Publications.")

Janet looks at her 2004 Estimated Tax Worksheet that is provided with Form 1040-ES. Unlike Schedule C and Schedule SE, Form 1040-ES isn't sent in with your annual 1040 tax return. Instead, you use the worksheet to calculate how much you estimate you'll owe in taxes. The tax payments are made with 1040-ES payment vouchers which are also included in the 1040-ES form booklet. Once you pay estimated taxes, the IRS will send you custom vouchers.

The simplest way to use your Estimated Tax Worksheet is to look at Line 14b and Line 14c. If you pay 100% of the tax you owed last year, you'll avoid a penalty. If your AGI is over $150,000, you must pay 110% of your last year's tax.

So, if you owed $8,000 in taxes last year, this means you would need to pay at least $8,000 this year in estimated taxes to avoid a penalty. If you pay $2,000 per quarterly installment, you'll be okay.

You can use last year's 1040 tax return to see your total taxes paid. Always keep copies of your tax returns. For *next* year (2005 here), Janet could use Line 62 of her 2004 Form 1040, showing a total tax bill of $8,409.16. If she paid this amount in quarterly installments, she'd avoid a penalty, even if her tax bill turned out to be much higher next year.

The method of just using Line 14b works if you anticipate having an income similar to last year's income. However, if your income drops significantly, you will pay more than necessary in estimated taxes, using this method. You will, of course, get that money refunded to you. But, some people don't like giving up the time value of money. And, you might find you need the money!

The other downside to just paying last year's tax as your estimated tax total is that, if your income shoots way up, you'll find you owe a lot more money at the end of the year. It can be very inconvenient to find yourself needing to come up with thousands of dollars by April 15. So, even if you don't pay the money to the IRS immediately, it's good to know about how much tax you'll owe next year.

We'll have Janet fill out the entire Estimated Tax Worksheet which comes with 1040-ES. (Note: We deleted the extra instructional pages from Form 1040-ES. We are only showing the Estimated Tax Worksheet and payment vouchers. If desired, you can download the full package "Form 1040-ES" from IRS.gov.)

Assume for 2004, Janet predicts she'll earn $50,000 in AGI. Line 1 is $50,000. This is only an estimate. Janet might only earn $44,000 or maybe $70,000. (Use last year's earnings to help estimate the upcoming year's earnings. You can multiply last year's earnings by any estimated growth you expect your business to have.)

On Line 2, we subtract Janet's standard deduction (or itemized deduction estimate) from her estimated AGI. Notice, only if your itemized deduction is larger than the standard deduction would you itemize, so it's safe to use the standard deduction. Using the standard deduction will lead to paying more in estimated taxes. Don't worry if you overpay your estimated taxes, you can receive a refund or have the credit applied to your estimated taxes for the next year. The important thing is to avoid penalties.)

Line 4 subtracts Janet's personal exemption of $3,100. Line 5 shows Janet's estimated taxable income. Line 6 calculates the tax on Line 5's estimated income. Here, Janet predicts she'll owe $7,250 in income taxes next year.

On Line 11, Janet estimates she'll owe $7,650 in self-employment taxes (15.3% of $50,000). Notice the instructions for Line 1 say you should subtract one-half of your self-employment tax when estimating your AGI, because you're allowed to deduct that from your income (Line 30 of the 1040). You can skip that step. It just means your estimated tax payments, based upon next year's income, will be slightly larger.

Line 13a shows Janet predicts she'll owe $14,900 in total taxes next year. Janet could just divide this amount by four and pay that quarterly as her estimated tax payments.

Line 14a simply calculates 90% of your estimated tax (here $13,410.00), because that's the minimum you must pay to avoid a penalty, *assuming you're paying an amount less than last year's total tax.*

Line 14b shows the tax paid on your last year's tax return. For next year, Janet would use Line 62 ($8,409.16) of her 1040.

Line 14c is the annual, estimated tax payment required to avoid a penalty. It is the *smaller* of 90% of Janet's estimated tax for the year or 100% of her tax bill for the previous year.

If you anticipate earning more money next year than last, you can simply pay one-quarter of your last year's total tax as your minimum estimated tax payment. For Janet, that would be $2,102.29.

If during the year, Janet finds her income will be less than last year's and she'd rather pay 90% of her estimated income instead of 100% of last year's tax, she could reduce her estimated tax payments. You don't need to pay the same amount every quarter. But, the conservative estimate is always to pay 100% of last year's tax.

You now understand estimated tax payments. To make her first estimated tax payment, Janet enters $2,102.29 on Payment Voucher 1 and pays this amount to the IRS. Janet could, of course, round this up to $2,103 or pay more. Once you start making estimated tax payments, the IRS will send you personalized payment vouchers listing your name and Social Security number. *Janet will also need to see if her state requires estimated tax payments.* See the state resources at the end of this book for more information about your state's taxing authority.

Next year, Janet might want to look into forming an IRA or a self-employed retirement account, such as an SEP, to reduce her taxable income. She might also want to examine the option of forming an S corporation to reduce her self-employment taxes.

For a sole proprietor (Schedule C business) or a single-member LLC (which for tax purposes is treated as a sole proprietorship), that's all there is to federal business taxes. Use Schedule C to report your business income. Use Schedule SE to calculate your self-employment tax. Use Schedule 1040-ES to make your estimated tax payments.

Profit or Loss From Business

(Sole Proprietorship)

▶ **Partnerships, joint ventures, etc., must file Form 1065 or 1065-B.**

▶ Attach to Form 1040 or 1041. ▶ See Instructions for Schedule C (Form 1040).

OMB No. 1545-0074

2004

Attachment
Sequence No. **09**

Name of proprietor	Social security number (SSN)
Janet	

A	Principal business or profession, including product or service (see page C-2 of the instructions)	**B** Enter code from pages C-7, 8, & 9 ▶

C	Business name. If no separate business name, leave blank.	**D** Employer ID number (EIN), if any
	Janet's Advertising Design	

E Business address (including suite or room no.) ▶ ....
City, town or post office, state, and ZIP code

F Accounting method: (1) ☐ Cash (2) ☑ Accrual (3) ☐ Other (specify) ▶ ....
G Did you "materially participate" in the operation of this business during 2004? If "No," see page C-3 for limit on losses ☑ Yes ☐ No
H If you started or acquired this business during 2004, check here . . . . ▶ ☐

Part I   Income

1	Gross receipts or sales. Caution. If this income was reported to you on Form W-2 and the "Statutory employee" box on that form was checked, see page C-3 and check here . . . . ▶ ☐	1	39000	00
2	Returns and allowances	2		
3	Subtract line 2 from line 1	3		
4	Cost of goods sold (from line 42 on page 2)	4	300	00
5	**Gross profit.** Subtract line 4 from line 3.	5	38700	00
6	Other income, including Federal and state gasoline or fuel tax credit or refund (see page C-3) . . .	6		
7	**Gross income.** Add lines 5 and 6 . . . . ▶	7	38700	00

Part II   Expenses. Enter expenses for business use of your home **only** on line 30.

8	Advertising	8			19 Pension and profit-sharing plans	19		
9	Car and truck expenses (see page C-3)	9			20 Rent or lease (see page C-5):			
10	Commissions and fees . .	10			a Vehicles, machinery, and equipment .	20a		
11	Contract labor (see page C-4)	11			b Other business property. . .	20b		
12	Depletion	12			21 Repairs and maintenance . .	21		
13	Depreciation and section 179 expense deduction (not included in Part III) (see page C-4)	13	1600	00	22 Supplies (not included in Part III)	22		
					23 Taxes and licenses	23		
					24 Travel, meals, and entertainment:			
					a Travel	24a		
14	Employee benefit programs (other than on line 19). .	14			b Meals and entertainment			
15	Insurance (other than health) .	15			c Enter nondeductible amount included on line 24b (see page C-5) .			
16	Interest:							
a	Mortgage (paid to banks, etc.) .	16a			d Subtract line 24c from line 24b	24d		
b	Other	16b			25 Utilities	25		
17	Legal and professional services	17			26 Wages (less employment credits) .	26		
18	Office expense	18			27 Other expenses (from line 48 on page 2)	27	1620	00

28	**Total expenses** before expenses for business use of home. Add lines 8 through 27 in columns . ▶	28	3220	00
29	Tentative profit (loss). Subtract line 28 from line 7	29	35480	00
30	Expenses for business use of your home. Attach Form 8829	30		
31	**Net profit or (loss).** Subtract line 30 from line 29.			
	• If a profit, enter on **Form 1040, line 12,** and **also** on **Schedule SE, line 2** (statutory employees, see page C-6). Estates and trusts, enter on Form 1041, line 3.	31	35480	00
	• If a loss, you **must** go to line 32.			

32	If you have a loss, check the box that describes your investment in this activity (see page C-6).		
	• If you checked 32a, enter the loss on **Form 1040, line 12,** and **also** on **Schedule SE, line 2** (statutory employees, see page C-6). Estates and trusts, enter on Form 1041, line 3.	32a ☐ All investment is at risk.	
	• If you checked 32b, you **must** attach **Form 6198.**	32b ☐ Some investment is not at risk.	

For Paperwork Reduction Act Notice, see Form 1040 instructions. Cat. No. 11334P Schedule C (Form 1040) 2004

Part III   Cost of Goods Sold (see page C-6)

33   Method(s) used to
value closing inventory: **a** ☑ Cost   **b** ☐ Lower of cost or market   **c** ☐ Other (attach explanation)

34   Was there any change in determining quantities, costs, or valuations between opening and closing inventory? If
"Yes," attach explanation . . . .   ☐ Yes   ☑ No

35 Inventory at beginning of year. If different from last year's closing inventory, attach explanation . .	35	0
36 Purchases less cost of items withdrawn for personal use	36	3000
37 Cost of labor. Do not include any amounts paid to yourself	37	
38 Materials and supplies	38	
39 Other costs	39	
40 Add lines 35 through 39	40	3000
41 Inventory at end of year	41	2700
42 **Cost of goods sold.** Subtract line 41 from line 40. Enter the result here and on page 1, line 4 . .	42	300

Part IV   Information on Your Vehicle. Complete this part **only** if you are claiming car or truck expenses o
line 9 and are not required to file Form 4562 for this business. See the instructions for line 13 on pag
C-4 to find out if you must file Form 4562.

43   When did you place your vehicle in service for business purposes? (month, day, year) ▶ ..../........./........ .

44   Of the total number of miles you drove your vehicle during 2004, enter the number of miles you used your vehicle for:

a   Business .... **b** Commuting .... **c** Other ....

45   Do you (or your spouse) have another vehicle available for personal use?. . . . . ☐ Yes   ☐ No

46   Was your vehicle available for personal use during off-duty hours?   . . . . ☐ Yes   ☐ No

47a Do you have evidence to support your deduction?   . . . . ☐ Yes   ☐ No

b   If "Yes," is the evidence written? . . . . ☐ Yes   ☐ No

Part V   Other Expenses. List below business expenses not included on lines 8–26 or line 30.

Shipping/Freight	200	0
Paper, Stationary	500	0
Postage	400	0
Telephone	500	0
Desktop Publishing Today (Magazine Subscription)	20	0
(A separate sheet of paper could be used if there were more expenses.)		
48 **Total other expenses.** Enter here and on page 1, line 27	48	1620 0

SCHEDULE SE (Form 1040) Department of the Treasury Internal Revenue Service	**Self-Employment Tax** ▶ Attach to Form 1040. ▶ See Instructions for Schedule SE (Form 1040).	OMB No. 1545-0074 **2004** Attachment Sequence No. **17**

Name of person with **self-employment** income (as shown on Form 1040) Janet	Social security number of person with **self-employment** income ▶	

Who Must File Schedule SE

You must file Schedule SE if:

● You had net earnings from self-employment from **other than** church employee income (line 4 of Short Schedule SE or line 4c of Long Schedule SE) of $400 or more **or**

● You had church employee income of $108.28 or more. Income from services you performed as a minister or a member of a religious order **is not** church employee income (see page SE-1).

Note. Even if you had a loss or a small amount of income from self-employment, it may be to your benefit to file Schedule SE and use either "optional method" in Part II of Long Schedule SE (see page SE-3).

Exception. If your only self-employment income was from earnings as a minister, member of a religious order, or Christian Science practitioner **and** you filed Form 4361 and received IRS approval not to be taxed on those earnings, **do not** file Schedule SE. Instead, write "Exempt–Form 4361" on Form 1040, line 57.

May I Use Short Schedule SE or Must I Use Long Schedule SE?

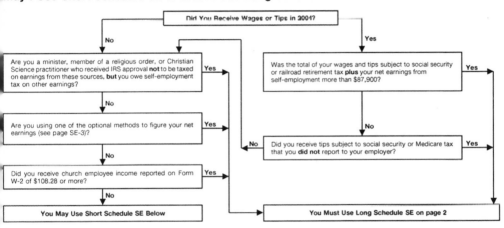

Section A—Short Schedule SE. Caution. Read above to see if you can use Short Schedule SE.

1	Net farm profit or (loss) from Schedule F, line 36, and farm partnerships, Schedule K-1 (Form 1065), box 14, code A	**1**	
2	Net profit or (loss) from <u>Schedule C</u>, line 31; Schedule C-EZ, line 3; Schedule K-1 (Form 1065), box 14, code A (other than farming); and Schedule K-1 (Form 1065-B), box 9. Ministers and members of religious orders, see page SE-1 for amounts to report on this line. See page SE-2 for other income to report	**2**	35480 | 00
3	Combine lines 1 and 2	**3**	35480 | 00
4	**Net earnings from self-employment.** Multiply line 3 by 92.35% (.9235). If less than $400, **do not** file this schedule; you do not owe self-employment tax . . . . ▶	**4**	32765 | 78
5	**Self-employment tax.** If the amount on line 4 is: ● $87,900 or less, multiply line 4 by 15.3% (.153). Enter the result here and on **Form 1040, line 57.** ● More than $87,900, multiply line 4 by 2.9% (.029). Then, add $10,899.60 to the result. Enter the total here and on **Form 1040, line 57.**	**5**	5013 | 16
6	**Deduction for one-half of self-employment tax.** Multiply line 5 by 50% (.5). Enter the result here and on **Form 1040, line 30**	**6**	2506 | 58

For Paperwork Reduction Act Notice, see Form 1040 instructions.　　　　Cat. No. 11358Z　　　　**Schedule SE (Form 1040) 2004**

Form **1040** Department of the Treasury—Internal Revenue Service

U.S. Individual Income Tax Return **2004** (99) IRS Use Only—Do not write or staple in this space.

For the year Jan. 1–Dec. 31, 2004, or other tax year beginning , 2004, ending , 20

OMB No. 1545-0074

Label
(See instructions on page 16.)

Use the IRS label. Otherwise, please print or type.

L A B E L   H E R E

Your first name and initial: **Janet** | Last name | Your social security number

If a joint return, spouse's first name and initial | Last name | Spouse's social security numb

Home address (number and street). If you have a P.O. box, see page 16. | Apt. no.

City, town or post office, state, and ZIP code. If you have a foreign address, see page 16.

▲ **Important!** ▲
You **must** enter your SSN(s) above.

Presidential Election Campaign (See page 16.)
▶ Note. Checking "Yes" will not change your tax or reduce your refund.
Do you, or your spouse if filing a joint return, want $3 to go to this fund? . . . ▶

You | Spouse
☐ Yes ☐ No ☐ Yes ☐ N

Filing Status

Check only one box.

1 ☑ Single
2 ☐ Married filing jointly (even if only one had income)
3 ☐ Married filing separately. Enter spouse's SSN above and full name here. ▶
4 ☐ Head of household (with qualifying person). (See page 17.) the qualifying person is a child but not your dependent, ent this child's name here. ▶
5 ☐ Qualifying widow(er) with dependent child (see page 17

Exemptions

6a ☑ **Yourself.** If someone can claim you as a dependent, **do not** check box 6a . . . .
b ☐ **Spouse** . . . .

If more than four dependents, see page 18.

c **Dependents:**

(1) First name Last name	(2) Dependent's social security number	(3) Dependent's relationship to you	(4)☑ if qualifying child for child tax credit (see page 18)
			☐
			☐
			☐
			☐

d Total number of exemptions claimed . . . .

Boxes checked on 6a and 6b
No. of children on 6c who:
• lived with you
• did not live with you due to divorce or separation (see page 18)
Dependents on 6c not entered above

Add numbers on lines above ▶ **1**

Income

Attach Form(s) W-2 here. Also attach Forms W-2G and 1099-R if tax was withheld.

If you did not get a W-2, see page 19.

Enclose, but do not attach, any payment. Also, please use Form 1040-V.

7	Wages, salaries, tips, etc. Attach Form(s) W-2	7	
8a	**Taxable** interest. Attach Schedule B if required	8a	
b	**Tax-exempt** interest. **Do not** include on line 8a . . .	8b		
9a	Ordinary dividends. Attach Schedule B if required	9a	
b	Qualified dividends (see page 20)	9b		
10	Taxable refunds, credits, or offsets of state and local income taxes (see page 20) .	10	
11	Alimony received	11	
12	Business income or (loss). Attach Schedule C or C-EZ	12	35480	0
13	Capital gain or (loss). Attach Schedule D if required. If not required, check here ▶ ☐	13	
14	Other gains or (losses). Attach Form 4797	14	
15a	IRA distributions . 15a	b Taxable amount (see page 22)	15b	
16a	Pensions and annuities 16a	b Taxable amount (see page 22)	16b	
17	Rental real estate, royalties, partnerships, S corporations, trusts, etc. Attach Schedule E	17	
18	Farm income or (loss). Attach Schedule F	18	
19	Unemployment compensation	19	
20a	Social security benefits 20a	b Taxable amount (see page 24)	20b	
21	Other income. List type and amount (see page 24)	21	
22	Add the amounts in the far right column for lines 7 through 21. This is your **total income** ▶	22	35480	0

Adjusted Gross Income

23	Educator expenses (see page 26)	23	
24	Certain business expenses of reservists, performing artists, and fee-basis government officials. Attach Form 2106 or 2106-EZ	24	
25	IRA deduction (see page 26)	25	
26	Student loan interest deduction (see page 28) . . .	26	
27	Tuition and fees deduction (see page 29)	27	
28	Health savings account deduction. Attach Form 8889 . .	28	
29	Moving expenses. Attach Form 3903	29	
30	One-half of self-employment tax. Attach Schedule SE .	30	2506	58
31	Self-employed health insurance deduction (see page 30)	31	
32	Self-employed SEP, SIMPLE, and qualified plans . . .	32	
33	Penalty on early withdrawal of savings	33	
34a	Alimony paid b Recipient's SSN ▶	34a	
35	Add lines 23 through 34a	35	2506	58
36	Subtract line 35 from line 22. This is your **adjusted gross income** . . . . . ▶	36	32973	42

For Disclosure, Privacy Act, and Paperwork Reduction Act Notice, see page 75. Cat. No. 11320B Form **1040** (2004

Tax and Credits	37	Amount from line 36 (adjusted gross income)	37	32973 42

Standard Deduction for—

38a	Check if: [ ] **You** were born before January 2, 1940, [ ] Blind. [ ] **Spouse** was born before January 2, 1940, [ ] Blind. **Total boxes checked ▶ 38a**	
b	If your spouse itemizes on a separate return or you were a dual-status alien, see page 31 and check here ▶ 38b [ ]	

- **People who checked any box on line 38a or 38b or who can be claimed as a dependent,** see page 31.
- **All others:**

Single or Married filing separately, $4,850

Married filing jointly or Qualifying widow(er), $9,700

Head of household, $7,150

39	**Itemized deductions** (from Schedule A) **or** your **standard deduction** (see left margin) . .	39	4850	00
40	Subtract line 39 from line 37	40	28123	42
41	If line 37 is $107,025 or less, multiply $3,100 by the total number of exemptions claimed on line 6d. If line 37 is over $107,025, see the worksheet on page 33	41	3100	00
42	**Taxable income.** Subtract line 41 from line 40. If line 41 is more than line 40, enter -0-	42	25023	42
43	**Tax** (see page 33). Check if any tax is from: **a** [ ] Form(s) 8814 **b** [ ] Form 4972 . . .	43	3396	00
44	**Alternative minimum tax** (see page 35). Attach Form 6251	44		
45	Add lines 43 and 44 . . . . ▶	45	3396	00

46	Foreign tax credit. Attach Form 1116 if required	46	
47	Credit for child and dependent care expenses. Attach Form 2441	47	
48	Credit for the elderly or the disabled. Attach Schedule R . .	48	
49	Education credits. Attach Form 8863	49	
50	Retirement savings contributions credit. Attach Form 8880 . .	50	
51	Child tax credit (see page 37)	51	
52	Adoption credit. Attach Form 8839	52	
53	Credits from: **a** [ ] Form 8396 **b** [ ] Form 8859 . . .	53	
54	Other credits. Check applicable box(es): **a** [ ] Form 3800 **b** [ ] Form 8801 **c** [ ] Specify _____	54	

55	Add lines 46 through 54. These are your **total credits**	55		
56	Subtract line 55 from line 45. If line 55 is more than line 45, enter -0- . . . . . . ▶	56	3396	00

Other Taxes	57	Self-employment tax. Attach Schedule SE	57	5013 16

58	Social security and Medicare tax on tip income not reported to employer. Attach Form 4137 . .	58		
59	Additional tax on IRAs, other qualified retirement plans, etc. Attach Form 5329 if required .	59		
60	Advance earned income credit payments from Form(s) W-2	60		
61	Household employment taxes. Attach Schedule H	61		
62	Add lines 56 through 61. This is your **total tax** . . . . ▶	62	8409	16

Payments

If you have a qualifying child, attach Schedule EIC.

63	Federal income tax withheld from Forms W-2 and 1099 . .	63	
64	2004 estimated tax payments and amount applied from 2003 return	64	0 00
65a	**Earned income credit (EIC)**	65a	
b	Nontaxable combat pay election ▶	65b	
66	Excess social security and tier 1 RRTA tax withheld (see page 54)	66	
67	Additional child tax credit. Attach Form 8812	67	
68	Amount paid with request for extension to file (see page 54)	68	
69	Other payments from: **a** [ ] Form 2439 **b** [ ] Form 4136 **c** [ ] Form 8885 .	69	

70	Add lines 63, 64, 65a, and 66 through 69. These are your **total payments** . . . . ▶	70	0	00

Refund

Direct deposit? See page 54 and fill in 72b, 72c, and 72d.

71	If line 70 is more than line 62, subtract line 62 from line 70. This is the amount you **overpaid**	71		
72a	Amount of line 71 you want **refunded to you** . . . . ▶	72a		
▶ b	Routing number [ ] ▶ c Type: [ ] Checking [ ] Savings			
▶ d	Account number [ ]			
73	Amount of line 71 you want **applied to your 2005 estimated tax** ▶	73		

Amount You Owe

74	**Amount you owe.** Subtract line 70 from line 62. For details on how to pay, see page 55 ▶	74	8409	16
75	Estimated tax penalty (see page 55)	75		

Third Party Designee

Do you want to allow another person to discuss this return with the IRS (see page 56)? [ ] **Yes.** Complete the following. [ ] **No**

Designee's name ▶	Phone no. ▶ ( )	Personal identification number (PIN) ▶ [ ]

Sign Here

Joint return? See page 17.

Keep a copy for your records.

Under penalties of perjury, I declare that I have examined this return and accompanying schedules and statements, and to the best of my knowledge and belief, they are true, correct, and complete. Declaration of preparer (other than taxpayer) is based on all information of which preparer has any knowledge.

Your signature	Date	Your occupation	Daytime phone number ( )
Spouse's signature. If a joint return, **both** must sign.	Date	Spouse's occupation	

Paid Preparer's Use Only

Preparer's signature ▶	Date	Check if self-employed [ ]	Preparer's SSN or PTIN
Firm's name (or yours if self-employed), address, and ZIP code ▶		EIN	
		Phone no. ( )	

Form **1040** (2004)

Instructions for the 2004 Estimated Tax Worksheet

Line 1. Adjusted gross income. Use your 2003 tax return and instructions as a guide to figuring the adjusted gross income you expect in 2004 (but be sure to consider the **Changes Effective for 2004** that begin on page 1). For more details on figuring your adjusted gross income, see **Expected Adjusted Gross Income** in Pub. 505. If you are self-employed, be sure to take into account the deduction for one-half of your self-employment tax.

Line 8. Include on this line the additional taxes from **Form 4972,** Tax on Lump-Sum Distributions, or **Form 8814,** Parents' Election To Report Child's Interest and Dividends. Also include any recapture of education credits.

Line 9. Credits. See the instructions for the 2003 Form 1040, lines 44 through 52, or Form 1040A, lines 29 through 34. However, be sure to see **Certain credits no longer allowed against alternative minimum tax (AMT)** on page 1.

Line 11. Self-employment tax. If you and your spouse make joint estimated tax payments and you both have self-employment income, figure the self-employment tax for each

2004 Estimated Tax Worksheet (keep for your records)

1	Adjusted gross income you expect in 2004 (see instructions above)	**1**	50000	00
2	• If you plan to itemize deductions, enter the estimated total of your itemized deductions. **Caution:** *If line 1 above is over $142,700 ($71,350 if married filing separately), your deduction may be reduced. See Pub. 505 for details.* • If you do not plan to itemize deductions, enter your standard deduction from page 2.	**2**	4850	00
3	Subtract line 2 from line 1	**3**	45150	00
4	Exemptions. Multiply $3,100 by the number of personal exemptions. If you can be claimed as a dependent on another person's 2004 return, your personal exemption is not allowed. **Caution:** *See Pub. 505 to figure the amount to enter if line 1 above is over: $214,050 if married filing jointly or qualifying widow(er); $178,350 if head of household; $142,700 if single; or $107,025 if married filing separately*	**4**	3100	00
5	Subtract line 4 from line 3	**5**	42050	00
6	**Tax.** Figure your tax on the amount on line 5 by using the **2004 Tax Rate Schedules** on page 2. **Caution:** *If you have qualified dividends or a net capital gain, see Pub. 505 to figure the tax*	**6**	7250	00
7	Alternative minimum tax from Form 6251	**7**		
8	Add lines 6 and 7. Also include any tax from Forms 4972 and 8814 and any recapture of education credits (see instructions above)	**8**	7250	00
9	Credits (see instructions above). **Do not** include any income tax withholding on this line . . .	**9**		
10	Subtract line 9 from line 8. If zero or less, enter -0-	**10**	7250	00
11	Self-employment tax (see instructions above). Estimate of 2004 net earnings from self-employment $......50,000....... ; if **$87,900 or less,** multiply the amount by 15.3%; if **more than $87,900,** multiply the amount by 2.9%, add $10,899.60 to the result, and enter the total. **Caution:** *If you also have wages subject to social security tax, see Pub. 505 to figure the amount to enter*	**11**	7650	00
12	Other taxes (see instructions on page 5)	**12**		
13a	Add lines 10 through 12	**13a**	14900	00
b	Earned income credit, additional child tax credit, and credits from **Form 4136** and **Form 8885**	**13b**		
c	**Total 2004 estimated tax.** Subtract line 13b from line 13a. If zero or less, enter -0- . . . ▶	**13c**	14900	00

14a	Multiply line 13c by 90% (66⅔% for farmers and fishermen) . . .	**14a**	13410	00
b	Enter the tax shown on your 2003 tax return (110% of that amount if you are not a farmer or fisherman and the adjusted gross income shown on line 35 of that return is more than $150,000 or, if married filing separately for 2004, more than $75,000)	**14b**	8409	16
c	**Required annual payment to avoid a penalty.** Enter the **smaller** of line 14a or 14b . . . ▶	**14c**	8409	16

Caution: *Generally, if you do not prepay (through income tax withholding and estimated tax payments) at least the amount on line 14c, you may owe a penalty for not paying enough estimated tax. To avoid a penalty, make sure your estimate on line 13c is as accurate as possible. Even if you pay the required annual payment, you may still owe tax when you file your return. If you prefer, you may pay the amount shown on line 13c. For details, see Pub. 505.*

15	Income tax withheld and estimated to be withheld during 2004 (including income tax withholding on pensions, annuities, certain deferred income, etc.)	**15**		
16	Subtract line 15 from line 14c. (**Note:** *If zero or less or line 13c minus line 15 is less than $1,000, stop here. You are not required to make estimated tax payments.*)	**16**	8409	16
17	If the first payment you are required to make is due April 15, 2004, enter ¼ of line 16 (minus any 2003 overpayment that you are applying to this installment) here, and on your **payment voucher(s)** if you are paying by check or money order. (**Note:** *Household employers, see instructions on page 5.*)	**17**	2102	29

Record of Estimated Tax Payments (Farmers, fishermen, and fiscal year taxpayers, see page 2 for payment due dates.)

Payment number	Payment due date	(a) Date paid	(b) Check or money order number or credit card confirmation number	(c) Amount paid (do not include any credit card convenience fee)	(d) 2003 overpayment credit applied	(e) Total amount paid and credited (add (c) and (d))
1	4/15/2004					
2	6/15/2004					
3	9/15/2004					
4	1/18/2005*					
Total	. . . . ▶					

You do not have to make this payment if you file your 2004 tax return by January 31, 2005, **and** pay the entire balance due with your return.

Where To File Your Payment Voucher if Paying by Check or Money Order

Mail your payment voucher and check or money order to the Internal Revenue Service at the address shown below for the place where you live. **Do not** mail your tax return to this address or send an estimated tax payment without a payment voucher. Also, do not mail your estimated tax payments to the address shown in the Form 1040 or 1040A instructions. If you need more payment vouchers, use another Form 1040-ES package.

Note: *For proper delivery of your estimated tax payment to a P.O. box, you must include the box number in the address. Also, note that only the U.S. Postal Service can deliver to P.O. boxes.*

IF you live in . . .	THEN use . . .
Maine, Massachusetts, New Hampshire, New York, Vermont	P.O. Box 37001 Hartford, CT 06176-0001
Connecticut, District of Columbia, Maryland, New Jersey, Pennsylvania	P.O. Box 80102 Cincinnati, OH 45280-0002

Alabama, Florida, Georgia, Mississippi, North Carolina, Rhode Island, South Carolina, West Virginia	P.O. Box 105900 Atlanta, GA 30348-5900
Ohio, Virginia	P.O. Box 105225 Atlanta, GA 30348-5225
Delaware, Illinois, Indiana, Iowa, Kansas, Michigan, Minnesota, Missouri, Nebraska, North Dakota, South Dakota, Wisconsin	P.O. Box 970006 St. Louis, MO 63197-0006
Arizona, Utah	P.O. Box 1219 Charlotte, NC 28201-1219
Alaska, California, Hawaii, Idaho, Montana, Nevada, Oregon, Washington, Wyoming	P.O. Box 510000 San Francisco, CA 94151-5100
Arkansas, Colorado, Kentucky, Louisiana, New Mexico, Oklahoma, Tennessee, Texas	P.O. Box 660406 Dallas, TX 75266-0406

All APO and FPO addresses, American Samoa, the Commonwealth of the Northern Mariana Islands, nonpermanent residents of Guam or the Virgin Islands, Puerto Rico *(or if excluding income under Internal Revenue Code section 933)*, dual-status aliens, a foreign country; U.S. citizens and those filing Form 2555, 2555-EZ, or 4563 — P.O. Box 80102 Cincinnati, OH 45280-0002

Permanent residents of Guam* — Department of Revenue and Taxation Government of Guam P.O. Box 23607 GMF, GU 96921

Permanent residents of the Virgin Islands* — V.I. Bureau of Internal Revenue 9601 Estate Thomas Charlotte Amalie St. Thomas, VI 00802

* Permanent residents must prepare separate vouchers for estimated income tax and self-employment tax payments. Send the income tax vouchers to the address for permanent residents and the self-employment tax vouchers to the address for nonpermanent residents.

Tear off here

	Calendar year—Due Jan. 18, 2005	
File only if you are making a payment of estimated tax by check or money order. Mail this voucher with your check or money order payable to the **"United States Treasury."** Write your social security number and "2004 Form 1040-ES" on your check or money order. Do not send cash. Enclose, but do not staple or attach, your payment with this voucher.	Amount of estimated tax you are paying by check or money order.	Dollars / Cents

Your first name and initial	Your last name	Your social security number

If joint payment, complete for spouse

Spouse's first name and initial	Spouse's last name	Spouse's social security number

Address (number, street, and apt. no.)

City, state, and ZIP code. (If a foreign address, enter city, province or state, postal code, and country.)

For Privacy Act and Paperwork Reduction Act Notice, see instructions on page 5.

Form 1040-ES
Department of the Treasury
Internal Revenue Service

2004 Payment Voucher **3**

OMB No. 1545-0087

File only if you are making a payment of estimated tax by check or money order. Mail this voucher with your check or money order payable to the **"United States Treasury."** Write your social security number and "2004 Form 1040-ES" on your check or money order. Do not send cash. Enclose, but do not staple or attach, your payment with this voucher.

Calendar year—Due Sept. 15, 2004

Amount of estimated tax you are paying by check or money order.

Dollars	Cents

Type or print

Your first name and initial	Your last name	Your social security number

If joint payment, complete for spouse

Spouse's first name and initial	Spouse's last name	Spouse's social security number

Address (number, street, and apt. no.)

City, state, and ZIP code. (If a foreign address, enter city, province or state, postal code, and country.)

For Privacy Act and Paperwork Reduction Act Notice, see instructions on page 5.

- - - - - - - - - - - - - - Tear off here - - - - - - - - - - - - - -

Form 1040-ES
Department of the Treasury
Internal Revenue Service

2004 Payment Voucher **2**

OMB No. 1545-0087

File only if you are making a payment of estimated tax by check or money order. Mail this voucher with your check or money order payable to the **"United States Treasury."** Write your social security number and "2004 Form 1040-ES" on your check or money order. Do not send cash. Enclose, but do not staple or attach, your payment with this voucher.

Calendar year—Due June 15, 2004

Amount of estimated tax you are paying by check or money order.

Dollars	Cents

Type or print

Your first name and initial	Your last name	Your social security number

If joint payment, complete for spouse

Spouse's first name and initial	Spouse's last name	Spouse's social security number

Address (number, street, and apt. no.)

City, state, and ZIP code. (If a foreign address, enter city, province or state, postal code, and country.)

For Privacy Act and Paperwork Reduction Act Notice, see instructions on page 5.

- - - - - - - - - - - - - - Tear off here - - - - - - - - - - - - - -

Form 1040-ES
Department of the Treasury
Internal Revenue Service

2004 Payment Voucher **1**

OMB No. 1545-0087

File only if you are making a payment of estimated tax by check or money order. Mail this voucher with your check or money order payable to the **"United States Treasury."** Write your social security number and "2004 Form 1040-ES" on your check or money order. Do not send cash. Enclose, but do not staple or attach, your payment with this voucher.

Calendar year—Due April 15, 2004

Amount of estimated tax you are paying by check or money order.

Dollars	Cents
2102	29

Type or print

Your first name and initial	Your last name	Your social security number

If joint payment, complete for spouse

Spouse's first name and initial	Spouse's last name	Spouse's social security number

Address (number, street, and apt. no.)

City, state, and ZIP code. (If a foreign address, enter city, province or state, postal code, and country.)

For Privacy Act and Paperwork Reduction Act Notice, see instructions on page 5.

Chapter 9
Seven
Home-Based Business
Ideas

Here are seven home business ideas. These are specific businesses which can be operated from a home. I'm always amused at books that try to predict the hot jobs for the future. Leafing through one book, I saw "Underwater Archeologist." I'm not sure why that's a high-growth area, but I noticed the book failed to predict any Internet-based careers, such as web designer! The book didn't foresee the development of the Internet. Clearly, predicting the future isn't easy!

None of these businesses is earth-shattering. But, they all offer real opportunities for entrepreneurs, if the business matches the entrepreneur's personality and desires. We'll briefly describe the nature of the business, why the business provides value to clients or customers, and downsides to the particular business. Then, for the specific business you contemplate, we'll ask you to create a similar brief description of your proposed business idea.

1. Information Broker/Researcher

What they do: Information researchers and information professionals use their research skills to obtain information for individuals and companies. If you like studying and doing academic research, this might be the business for you. While many researchers spend considerable time on the Internet, most also spend substantial time at libraries, county courts, and other locations where various records are kept. Private investigators and skip tracers are one type of professional researcher.

Why the business provides value: People and companies value their time and often prefer to hire specialized individuals to do time-consuming jobs, like research. In some cases, people don't know how to go about collecting the information themselves. Companies and organizations can usually afford to spend the most on research.

Downsides: Like any consulting activity, this is a personal service which essentially limits income to billable hours. Many of the most lucrative opportunities, such as personal background checks for pre-employment screening, are already well-served by established companies.

Resources: *Building & Running a Successful Research Business: A Guide for the Independent Information Professional* by Mary Ellen Bates and Reva Basch.

2. Real Estate Investor/Manager

What they do: Real estate investors purchase real property for rent or resale.

Why the business provides value: Fixing up an older property can increase its value, so this is a possible opportunity for people who enjoy fixing up houses. For those who specialize in certain kinds of repairs or construction, contracting can also be lucrative, without requiring substantial investment in property. Many people who don't want to own homes choose to rent. So, you're providing the necessity of shelter.

Downsides: Real estate investment usually demands a significant capital investment. It's important to note that the early 2000s has been a time of greatly increasing property values. This means people could make money by just sitting on properties and reselling them at a later date. In a more subdued real estate market, this large gain in value doesn't occur as automatically. Further, if real estate prices drop, leveraged investors can lose substantial sums. Tenants can be problematic.

Resources: *Rental Houses for the Successful Small Investor* by Suzanne P. Thomas; *Real Estate Investing for Dummies* by Eric Tyson and Robert S. Griswold; *Investing in Real Estate, Fourth Edition* by Andrew James McLean and Gary W. Eldred; *Property Management for Dummies* by Robert S. Griswold. The website JohnTReed.com evaluates real estate courses.

3. Seminar Educator/Professional Speaker

What they do: Seminar instructors teach topics in which they're experts. For example, some people teach specialized classes about business taxation or preparing for the new SAT tests. Professional speakers often give keynote speeches at special events in front of large groups.

Why the business provides value: Seminar educators tend to be experts in their field and can offer students up-to-date information about a specialized area. I've never quite figured out why some organizations pay some individuals $10,000 plus per speech! (Entertainment value, I suppose.)

But, many organizations regularly pay $5,000 and up for competent and established professional speakers. Famous people earn far more, of course, with fees going well into six figures.

Downsides: Travel is usually required, because seldom can one region support many seminars in a specialized field. Plus, to give great seminars, you need to be an expert in your field. Building a reputation to earn big bucks giving keynote speeches usually takes time. Further, becoming a semi-celebrity isn't for everyone.

Many professional speakers sell their speaking services through speakers bureaus, which are like grocery stores for people who are looking for speakers. This means the speakers only talk. They aren't involved in planning the events. Speakers bureaus are sometimes involved in event planning. If you teach seminars, event planning skills may also be required.

Resources: *Marketing And Promoting Your Own Seminars And Workshops* by Fred Gleeck.

4. Financial Planner

What they do: Financial planners help clients plan their finances. Usually, they work with clients one-on-one to help them plan for retirement, college savings, and major purchases. They help clients select appropriate investments. Some money managers and mutual fund managers manage hundreds of millions of dollars in assets from their homes.

Why the business provides value: Many people who have solid incomes lack financial planning skills or don't have the time or the interest to handle all of their personal finances in a do-it-yourself fashion.

Downsides: Usually, solid credentials are required, such as being a Certified Financial Planner (CFP). Building a solid client base can take time. As with information professionals, this is a personal service which inherently limits income. One of the most popular types of financial planners today are flat-fee-based planners, who don't receive sales commissions. Many knowledgeable, affluent people simply index their money and wouldn't trust their money to an unestablished money manager.

Resources: *Getting Started As a Financial Planner* by Jeffrey H. Rattiner; *Networking With The Affluent And Their Advisors* by Thomas J. Stanley, Ph.D. Website: cfp.net.

5. Author/Publisher

What they do. Write and/or publish books. Other forms of publishing include newsletter publishing covering specialized topics and online publishing.

Why the business provides value. Books usually provide specialized information or entertainment value to readers. Newsletters and online publishing provide current information and analysis about a specialized field. Most smaller publishers serve a particular niche market, such as Christian readers, people interested in cooking, etc.

Downsides. This is a very competitive area with hundreds of thousands of books published each year. Newsletters must compete with magazines, the Internet, and other forms of communication.

Resources: *The Complete Guide to Self Publishing: Everything You Need to Know to Write, Publish, Promote, and Sell Your Own Book* by Tom Ross and Marilyn Ross; *The Publishing Game: Publish a Book in 30 Days* by Fern Reiss;

The Self-Publishing Manual: How to Write, Print and Sell Your Own Book by Dan Poynter; and *How To Start And Run A Small Book Publishing Company* by Peter Hupalo. The Publishers Marketing Association (pma-online.org) has classes about publishing.

6. Niche Online Retailer/eBay Seller

What they do: Niche retailers serve narrow market segments, usually a specialty area in which the business owner is interested. For example, "sporting goods" wouldn't be considered a niche. But, "golf supplies" or "tennis equipment" or "air gun supplies" would be a niche.

Some online sellers specialize in purchasing inventory at a discount and reselling it. But, unlike a catalog niche seller, the inventory tends to vary, based upon what the individual purchases at special bargain rates.

Why the business provides value: Niche sellers usually serve the most dedicated hobbyists, who spend considerable sums on their hobby or interest. Niche retailers often evaluate and recommend the best products and have specialized knowledge. Mail order and the Internet are key distribution and marketing channels, because many customers don't have local niche retail operations serving their interest.

Downsides: Many niche areas are well-served. Retailing involves carrying inventory, which represents a significant capital investment. There is inventory risk—the risk the inventory won't sell. Further, fulfillment of orders may be an issue for the home-based operator.

Resources: *Starting an Online Business for Dummies* by Greg Holden; *Starting an eBay Business for Dummies* by Marsha Collier; and *Building Your Business with Google For Dummies* by Brad Hill.

7. Auctioneer

What they do: According to the National Auctioneers Association, live auction sales in 2004 topped $217 billion. Art, antiques, and collectibles accounted for about $12 billion. You're probably familiar with auctions. Some quick-talking auctioneer gets bids for an item and sells the item to the highest bidder. Auctioneers help people and organizations sell things through auctions. For example, many larger estates have estate auctions, where property, including antiques, firearms, cars, motorcycles, and other personal valuables are sold at auction. Auctioneers help plan and advertise the auction.

Why the business provides value: Auctioneers help their clients get the best prices possible for items that would be time-consuming and more difficult to sell, if the sales were made individually.

Downsides: Travel is often involved. You're dependent upon a few key clients at any given time. Understanding the valuation of the property auctioned is essential. Appraiser is a related skill.

Resources: The National Auctioneers Association (NAA). Website: auctioneers.org.

For the home business idea you contemplate, write out statements for: 1) What your business does. You should be able to describe what you envision doing in only a sentence or two; 2) Why the business provides value to customers; and 3) Possible downsides to your business idea.

Chapter 10
Personal Finance And The
Home Business Entrepreneur

This chapter is written to give entrepreneurs a basic introduction to retirement planning and personal finance. How you manage your money will have a major impact upon the level of wealth you build. What matters most isn't what you earn, but what you're able to keep and save.

Unlike a larger entrepreneurial business, home businesses usually don't offer substantial sales value. In other words, you probably won't be selling your home business for a substantial profit. Instead, your home business will generate profits (some people call this cash flow), and you'll have those profits to invest over the years.

If you operate your home business full-time, it's likely you won't have a traditional pension or a 401(k) from regular employment to help fund your retirement. Thus, *retirement planning will be entirely in your hands.*

If you're younger and save, you have a powerful advantage working in your favor—the power of compound interest. I discuss compounding in detail in my book *Becoming An Investor: Building Wealth By Investing In Stocks, Bonds, And Mutual Funds.*

The only thing you really need to understand about compounding is that time is your ally, so you want to get started investing as early as possible. Even smaller amounts grow substantially if given enough time. *Eventually, the growth in interest and dividends on your invested capital will exceed the amount of money you save each year. This is the power of compounding.*

For example, assume you save and invest $10,000 each year. Assume you get a 10% rate of return on your investment. By the time you have $100,000 saved, just the interest, dividends, and growth in your existing portfolio matches your annual contribution.

By the time you have $250,000 saved, each year's growth contributes $25,000 to your portfolio. Modest contributions over fifteen years can lead to a portfolio worth $250,000. But, most people would have difficulty saving $25,000 per year. This is why it's much more difficult to build an adequate nest egg if you begin late.

Personal finance experts suggest you save and invest between 10% and 20% of your income. For the average investor, most of your retirement funds should be invested in low-cost mutual funds. I'd personally favor index funds, which purchase the broader stock market. You really don't need to know a great deal about the stock market or individual stocks to be successful. Just invest in diversified stock funds.

Retirement Accounts

You can open a brokerage account at a discount brokerage firm, such as Charles Schwab. The question becomes: What vehicle should you use for your retirement funds? In other words, what type of investment account should you open? Should you open a standard brokerage account? Should you open a traditional IRA or a Roth IRA? Or, should you open a tax-deferred account specially designed for small businesses, such as the SEP-IRA or the one-person 401(k)?

Tax-deferred accounts, such as the traditional IRA, a 401(k), and the SEP-IRA, allow you to save pre-tax dollars and allow tax-deferred compounding. This is a powerful advantage. This means contributions and growth aren't taxed until the money is withdrawn.

Today, however, many financial experts are somewhat less optimistic about traditional tax-deferred accounts for two reasons. First, today, tax rates are at historic lows. Second, the government is spending a lot more money than it's raising in tax revenue. This means the federal deficit is growing (it's actually evidence that tax rates are *too* low). Because of this, many experts believe that tax rates must invariably increase in the future. Some expect substantial tax increases.

Thus, putting aside income today to be taxed tomorrow *might* not be the wisest move. With this in mind, two vehicles look particularly attractive to me.

First, the Roth IRA. Contributions to the Roth IRA have already been taxed. The government promises that future withdrawals will be tax-free (the whole idea of the Roth IRA). Of course, the government could always renege on this pledge and decide to tax Roth withdrawals. However, it seems worth the risk. *The Roth IRA is particularly attractive to younger workers.*

Second, a standard brokerage account holding index funds. A standard brokerage account won't benefit from tax-deferred compounding, but with the low tax rates today, sacrificing tax-deferred compounding might be acceptable, given the predictions for future tax rates.

For those who wish to use tax-deferred retirement accounts, the new one-person 401(k) looks particularly attractive, if you wish to maximize the amount you can save tax deferred. Any small business owner *without employees* can set one up. If you anticipate hiring employees, I'd avoid the one-person 401(k), because, as soon as you have employees, you need to understand the reporting requirements of a conventional 401(k) and the eligibility rules affecting employees. *In fact, because of reporting and employee eligibility issues, if you have employees, you need to learn a lot more about the various retirement accounts, so you don't run afoul of the law.*

Another popular tax-deferred retirement account for small businesses is the SEP-IRA. And, of course, you could open a traditional, personal IRA.

For more information about the various tax-deferred retirement accounts available to small business owners, I recommend *Minding Her Own Business: The Self-Employed Woman's Essential Guide to Taxes and Financial Records* by Jan Zobel.

Day-To-Day Personal Finance

As discussed in Chapter 1, I'd use a financial program, such as Quicken, to better understand and categorize your personal expenses. You really need to know where you spend your money each month. You need to know the minimum income you need each month to cover your necessary expenses.

As your business becomes more established, if you move entirely to self-employment, I'd recommend building a financial reserve of at least three months income (six months would be better) held in a money market fund.

Be aware of the fluctuations in your business income. And, most crucially, as I mentioned before, it's usually not wise to risk savings to cover living expenses during the time you're starting a home-based business. Invest time, rather than money, whenever possible. For most new home businesses, this means starting part-time.

There are many good books to help you learn more about personal finance. I'd recommend starting with these books: *All Your Worth: The Ultimate Lifetime Money Plan* by Elizabeth Warren and Amelia Warren Tyagi (Elizabeth Warren is a professor at Harvard Law School and the leading expert on the financial problems the middle class face. If you're struggling financially, start with this book.); *Personal Finance For Dummies* by Eric Tyson (You can count on Tyson to provide solid financial advice.); *Making The Most Of Your Money* by Jane Bryant Quinn (I'm told a new edition is coming out. This is the most complete and best introduction to personal finance I've seen.); *The Money Book for the Young, Fabulous and Broke* by Suze Orman (The Old, Ordinary, and Rich don't tend to read Suze as much. But, she makes personal finance fun, and her ideas are *generally* good.)

As a business owner, you have maximum control over your future. But, you also have full responsibility for preparing for your retirement and managing your personal finances in a way that will allow you to achieve your dreams. You'll need to devote some attention to learning more about basic personal finance, if you're unfamiliar with the area.

Chapter 11
Fifteen Basic Steps In Starting
A Home-Based Business

1. Choose a business structure. If you're the sole owner of your company and form no other business structure, you'll be a sole proprietorship by default. This means you'll fill out IRS Schedule C (or C-EZ) and send it in with your IRS 1040 tax return. If you operate as a sole proprietor, order a copy of IRS Publication 334, which discusses Schedule C businesses in more detail. Other business structures to consider are the LLC and the S-Corporation.

2. Decide what your company will do. Use the basic business analysis you learned in the business model chapter. Decide upon your product, its price, and how you will market it. Create samples of your product or try to flesh out the details of your product or service.

3. Choose a business name that reflects the nature of your company. File a DBA (Doing Business As) statement with your state. This will allow you to operate your business legally under the "fictitious" name. See the state resources at the end of this book to learn how to register your DBA name. Sole proprietors, limited liability companies, and corporations can all have DBA names.

4. After receiving your assumed name certificate, open a business checking account in your company's name. Separating your business expenses and business income from your personal expenses and personal income will make it easier to manage your company. Try to select a bank with low fees.

5. If you expect to receive business mail, open a Post Office Box at your neighborhood post office. Don't get a very big box— not yet. If you receive a large volume of mail, the USPS will hold it outside the box and give it to you when you come in.

6. If you expect to receive a significant number of business phone calls, arrange to have a second phone number for your company. Adding a second hard-wired line is easy. As a general rule, you shouldn't mix business phones with personal phones. Depending upon your business, it may be useful or necessary for your business to have a cell phone number.

7. If you will be networking for business, have some professional business cards printed. You could also have some professional stationery printed or just design some on your PC. Depending upon your business, decide if other marketing materials should be produced, such as fliers. Possibly, you should create a website or hire a freelancer to create one for you.

8. Make a list of office supplies you require. For example, maybe you need a fax machine, a PC computer, a printer, a desk, and an ergonomic chair. Once you order from office supply companies, such as Quill (Quill.com) or Viking Office Products (Viking.com), you'll receive catalogs of their other products. Other great sources of office supplies include: Office Depot (OfficeDepot.com) and Office Max (OfficeMax.com).

9. If you'll be selling products subject to your state's sales tax, register with your state for a sales tax permit. This will

allow you to make taxable sales within your state. If you're selling to customers outside your state, in general, you don't have to collect sales tax. However, check with your state, because some states have special agreements with neighboring states requiring sales tax collection for sales made to the neighboring state. See the state-specific resources at the end of this book for more information about registering for sales tax.

10. See if your state provides free pamphlets, books, information packages, or other materials to help entrepreneurs starting a new business in your state. Often, state government provides a wealth of free help. Try to learn about your industry. See what industry-specific information you can dig up on the Internet or in books. See what associations serve businesses in your industry.

11. Begin marketing your product and make your first sale. Begin evaluating your business and marketing strategy to determine if you need to adjust your marketing methods. This is an important time of learning. Sometimes, what you envisioned won't work exactly, but with modifications your business will become successful. Use real world feedback to adjust your business and marketing strategies. Spend some time learning about the marketing methods that seem most appropriate to your business. The resource section at the end of this book lists some great marketing books.

12. Record your first sale. When in doubt, it's better to record too much information than too little. For example, you might make a journal that records: the customer's name; the product sold; the price charged; whether the customer paid in full or must be invoiced; etc. Ideally, this information will be transferred from a journal into a computer-based accounting program, such as Quicken, MYOB, or Peachtree Accounting. Always keep source documents related to your sales. You can

create separate folders to file away sales information for past months, quarters, or the year, whatever works best for you.

13. Evaluate the paper trail of incoming orders and the information you are recording in your accounting system. Is there anything you aren't recording that you should be recording? Keeping source documents allows you to enter information from past sales that you later decide is useful.

14. When you start making adequate profits so that you'll need to pay estimated taxes, register to pay estimated federal taxes. You might also need to register to pay estimated state taxes. Many states have simple forms you can send in with your estimated tax payment.

15. At the end of your first quarter (or month), use your computer accounting program to generate a report to see how well you're doing. Evaluate income, expenses, and profits. Create a balance sheet and create a profit and loss statement for your company. See what your profit margin is. What are your biggest expenses? How well are you doing? Try to learn from your accounting data how to improve your company. Order a copy of *Keeping The Books: Basic Record-Keeping and Accounting For The Small Business* by Linda Pinson and Jerry Jinnett for more information (business-plan.com).

Congratulations! You're now well on your way to starting and running your own home-based business!

Chapter 12
A State-By-State Resource Guide For Starting Your Business

A Research Primer

Government resources on the Internet are one of your best sources for current information about starting a business in your state. For online links to state-by-state business resources, please visit thinkinglike.com and follow the link titled "State-by-State Resources," where I've collected some small business links.

It's important to note that federal, state, county, local, and city websites are constantly revised (your tax dollars at work!), so specific web pages disappear regularly or are renamed. When in doubt, begin your online hunt for state-specific information by using google.com to search for your state's name and keywords related to the information you need to find.

For example, if you're looking for information about business licensing and permits in California, search "California business licenses" and similar expressions. If you're looking for information about registering your certificate of assumed name in Nevada, search expressions such as "Nevada business registration."

Another handy Internet research technique is working backward from a website URL that once was valid, but that can no longer be found. Delete specific pages and directories from the right and work toward the core of the web address. You might find the website still exists, but the specific page has been renamed.

For example, the web page www.state.in.us/sic/owners/appendb.html contains links to county recorder offices in the state of Indiana where you can register your certificate of assumed name.

If that web page fails, try entering "www.state.in.us/sic/owners/" in your web browser and see if a page can be found. If that fails, try entering "http://www.state.in.us" and see if the website still exists. Sometimes, you'll find the same information is available on the same website, but just under a different page.

When you want to locate government business information, it's sometimes useful to just enter your state's name into google.com and visit the state's web page. Then, seek links to business information. Some states are better than others at providing an abundance of material about starting a business. And, unfortunately, a few state websites are poorly organized.

If you know the name of the government agency you're trying to locate, searching google for the name of the agency will usually find it for you, even if you've forgotten the web address.

For example, if you're looking for "The Minnesota Department of Trade and Economic Development," you'll learn that in 2003 it merged with the "Minnesota Department of Economic Security" to become the "Minnesota Department of Employment and Economic Development." And, of course, it adopted a new web domain.

Be sure whenever you're redirected to a more current site that you bookmark the new site. Some states are better than others at supporting older web pages with a redirect page.

When you find websites, be careful they are, in fact, the state's true website or a legitimate, informational site. As a general rule, all state information is free and state sites have toll-free and local phone numbers where you can call the agency directly. Be careful about providing personal information over the Internet or to unknown parties.

If you find your state's home page, it often has a link to business information. I'd recommend bookmarking sites that you find provide useful business information.

As a new business owner, you're looking for three main things.

First, you need to find the agency that records business names. Usually, it's the secretary of state (or equivalent office) that records business registrations and certificates of assumed name. When you register a new business structure, such as an LLC or a corporation, you'll do it with this agency. Similarly, if you operate as a sole proprietor and you wish to file a DBA (Doing Business As) or certificate of assumed name, you'll probably do it with this agency. Many states register DBA names with the local county clerk or similar office, rather than with a state agency.

Second, you need to find the agency or agencies that regulate and license businesses. You'll probably have local licenses, so if you search google for the home page of your city, county, or municipality, you might find specific licensing information for your region.

Some states now offer "licensing wizards" to help you learn about specific business licenses that might apply to you. See the discussion under "California" later in this chapter for more information about how these licensing wizards typically work.

As discussed in the chapter about business licenses, if you operate in a regulated industry, you'll also be required to obtain specialized licenses. A state agency, usually called something like "The Board of Business and Professional Regulation," administers these specific licenses. Often, searching for the state's department of commerce will help you find the agency.

Third, you'll need to find the state agency that will collect your state taxes (Really. If you don't find them, they'll find you!). If you require a seller's permit, need to collect and pay sales tax, need to pay state estimated taxes, or want to understand state business taxation issues, this is the agency to contact. Often, this agency will go under the name "Department of Revenue." If you operate as a sole proprietor, you usually won't have to specifically register your business with the taxing agency (unless you collect state sales tax).

In addition to the agencies that monitor business names, administer licenses, and collect tax dollars, all states have Small Business Development Centers (SBDCs) which provide information and assist new business owners. Again, be sure the SBDC is state-sponsored and recognized. SBDCs are often associated with local colleges and universities.

http://sbdcnet.utsa.edu/default.htm
Provides links to Small Business Development Centers in each state.

Finally, most states provide an abundance of free information about starting a business in their state. Often, this free information will be in the form of a book or a downloadable pdf file, often made available from the department of commerce.

These free state books are your best source of information about starting a business in your state. Never ignore the valuable resources your state provides! A quick download, e-mail, or phone call will get you the free guide about starting a business in your state. I recommend you have a highlighter handy when reading these guides, because among the valuable information will be much information about things that won't concern you!

State Small Business Resources (United States)

Business Utility Zone Gateway
http://www.buzgate.org
(A "Knowledge Institute" project that contains links to many state resources, including private resources.)

Alabama

Alabama Department of Revenue
http://www.ador.state.al.us/bus.html
Telephone: 334-242-1170

Alabama Department of Revenue, Business Licensing
http://www.ador.state.al.us/licenses/index.html

Alaska

Alaska Dept of Commerce, Community, and Economic Development
http://www.dced.state.ak.us

http://www.dced.state.ak.us/occ/buslic.htm
Alaska Business License Program
Telephone: Juneau   907-465-2550
             Anchorage   907-269-8173

http://www.state.ak.us/local/bus1.html
Contains many resources including a link to the free pdf book "Starting a Small Business in Alaska."

Alaska Small Business Development Center
http://www.aksbdc.org

Arizona

Arizona Department of Commerce
http://www.azcommerce.com
1700 W. Washington, Suite 600
Phoenix, AZ 85007
Telephone: Phoenix Metro   602-771-1100
Telephone: Statewide   800-528-8421

From azcommerce.com, go to "Small Business Services" and then to "Arizona Business Connection" link. It has a step-by-step guide to starting your business in Arizona.

Arizona Department of Revenue
http://www.revenue.state.az.us

Arizona Business Licensing Guide
http://www.revenue.state.az.us/609/licensingguide.htm

Arkansas

Arkansas Small Business Development Center
http://asbdc.ualr.edu

http://www.accessarkansas.org/dfa/taxes/new_bus.html
Tax guide for starting a new business in Arkansas.

http://www.state.ar.us
This site has a link to "Business Resources" which has a link to "Local Government Search" to help you find local and city business licensing information.

California

Starting a Business in California From The Secretary Of State
http://www.ss.ca.gov/business/resources.htm
The above site has a link to:
http://www.calgold.ca.gov
This is a California business licensing search wizard. To use this feature, select your type of business. For example, "Vending Machine Operator." Then, select your county. For example, "Butte County." Then, select your city. For example, "Biggs." Then the site will display a detailed list of the licenses you must consider.

For example, for a Biggs City, Butte County, vending machine operator, we're told we need to look into getting a general business license from Biggs City Hall (contact information is provided), and we need to register our fictitious name with the Butte County Clerk (contact information also provided). Print out the list you generate. That way if the state comes back and says you should have registered for so-and-so, and it's not on the list, you can say, "Well, but, ah, it wasn't on the list!"

California Board of Equalization
http://www.boe.ca.gov
Telephone: 1-800-400-7115
This is equivalent to the Department of Revenue in most states. The Board of Equalization (sounds just a bit socialist to me!) has information about taxation, including sales tax and how to apply for a seller's permit.

Colorado

Colorado Small Business Development Center
http://www.state.co.us/oed/sbdc/

Colorado Secretary of State Business Center
http://www.sos.state.co.us/pubs/business/main.htm
Has a checklist publication for starting a business in Colorado.

Telephone: Colorado Business Center: 303-894-2200

Connecticut

Connecticut State Homepage
http://www.ct.gov
Has a link to "Doing Business In Connecticut," which includes
a guide to starting a business and to business regulation.

Connecticut Licensing Info Center
http://www.ct-clic.com
Telephone: Connecticut Business Response Center: 1-800-
392-2122
From the website: "A business information specialist can
answer your questions and send you an information package."

Delaware

Delaware Department of Revenue
http://www.state.de.us/revenue/services/BusServices.shtml
This page has links to "Establishing A Business In Delaware"
and "Incorporating In Delaware."
Telephone: Information about business licenses: 302-577-
8238

Sole proprietors in Delaware must complete a form: Sole
Proprietor Business License Application, Form 2301SP9703.

Florida

Florida Department of Revenue
http://sun6.dms.state.fl.us/dor/businesses/
Has a link to a free pdf book "New Business Owner's Guide."
Florida Department of Business and Professional Regulation
http://www.state.fl.us/dbpr/index.shtml
Licensing information for regulated professions.

Georgia

Georgia Secretary of State
http://www.sos.state.ga.us
Telephone: 404-656-7061
Outside of Metro Atlanta: 1-800-656-4558

http://www.georgia.gov
Has a link to Business and Professional Licensing.
Professional Licensing Boards Division
Telephone: 478-207-1300

First Stop Business Information Center
http://www.sos.state.ga.us/firststop/
Information about starting a business in Georgia.

Hawaii

State of Hawaii
Department of Business, Economic Development, and Tourism
P.O. Box 2359
Honolulu, Hawaii 96804
Telephone: 808-586-2423

Department of Commerce and Consumer Affairs
http://www.state.hi.us/dcca/
Has a link to business registration and licensing.

Department of Commerce and Consumer Affairs
Business Registration Division
Commissioner of Securities
P. O. Box 40
Honolulu, Hawaii 96810
Telephone: 808-586-2744
(Toll-free numbers for the various islands are given on the
website.)

Hawaii Small Business Development Center
http://www.hawaii-sbdc.org

Idaho

Idaho Business Portal
http://business.idaho.gov
This site has information about registering and licensing a
business in Idaho. The site has a regulatory requirements
wizard. For example, if you're starting a "sales" business, enter
that and it asks for more information. Tell it you're starting an
"Internet business," and it provides information about the
licensing requirements.

Idaho Secretary of State (assumed name registration)
http://www.idsos.state.id.us
Telephone: Secretary of State   208-334-2300

Idaho Small Business Development Center
http://www.idahobizhelp.org

Idaho Bureau of Professional Licensing
http://www2.state.id.us/ibol
Telephone: 208-334-3233
(Only a few specific home-business entrepreneurs, such as real
estate appraisers and athletic trainers, will be subject to
professional licensing.)

Lewis-Clark State College (Idaho SBDC)
http://www.lcsc.edu/isbdc/

Illinois

Illinois Department of Commerce
http://www.commerce.state.il.us

Illinois Small Business Help
http://www.illinoisbiz.biz
Look under "small business" to find a "Step-by-Step Guide to Starting a Business in Illinois."

Illinois Secretary of State (Business Registration)
http://www.sos.state.il.us
Telephone: 1-800-252-8980

Illinois First Stop Business Information Center
1-800-252-2923
Free *Starting A Business In Illinois Handbook*. The book is also available from Small Business Development Centers in the state.

Indiana

Business Owner's Guide To State Government
http://www.state.in.us/sic/owners/
Has details about name registration and business licensing.
Telephone: State Information Center: 317-233-0800 (for current license and permit requirements of your new business.)

Indiana Department of Revenue
http://www.IN.gov/dor

Indiana Small Business Development Center
http://www.isbdc.org/

Assumed names must be recorded with the county recorder. County recorder offices are listed in the Business Owner's Guide mentioned above.
(http://www.state.in.us/sic/owners/appendb.html)

Iowa

Iowa Business Network
http://www.iabusnet.org
(Iowa State University's College of Business SBDC)

Iowa Business Taxes (Department of Revenue)
http://www.state.ia.us/tax/business/business.html

Iowa Department of Economic Development
http://www.iowalifechanging.com/business/
Telephone: 1-515-242-4715
Telephone: 800-532-1215
E-mail: business@iowalifechanging.com
(Website has a link to Iowa's Business License Information Center.)

Iowa Secretary of State
Telephone: 515-281-5204 (for registering corporations)
Sole proprietors should contact their local county recorder office.

Starting A Business In Iowa (Department of Revenue)
http://www.state.ia.us/tax/business/newbus.html

Kansas

Operating A Business In Kansas
http://www.accesskansas.org/operating/

Kansas Department of Commerce
http://kdoch.state.ks.us
(See: Starting a Business -- First Stop Clearinghouse. Also has a pdf book *A Guide to Starting a Business in Kansas.*)

Kansas Secretary of State (Business Registration)
http://www.kssos.org
Telephone: 785-296-4564

Kansas Department of Revenue (Business Tax Registration)
http://www.kdor.state.ks.us
Telephone: 785-368-8222

Kentucky

Kentucky's Main Page has a link to business information.
http://www.thinkkentucky.com/

Kentucky Secretary of State
http://www.sos.state.ky.us/
(This site has a link to a "one-stop business license program" which helps entrepreneurs discover what business permits and licenses they need.)

Telephone: Kentucky Secretary of State: 502-564-2848
(Sole proprietors don't need to file with the Secretary of State. But, assumed name filings with the county clerk are required.)

Louisiana

Louisiana Secretary of State
http://www.sec.state.la.us
Telephone: 225-922-2675
(The Secretary of State has an online form you can fill out to get a checklist of the permits, licenses, and registrations you need. After filling out the form, you're e-mailed a description

of the licenses you need.)

Louisiana Department of Economic Development
http://www.lded.state.la.us

Maine

Maine Business Information Portal
http://www.maine.gov/portal/business/
(General licenses are managed at the city and town level. The
site has a link to city/town information.)

Maine Business Answers
http://www.maine.gov/businessanswers/
E-mail: business.answers@maine.gov
Telephone: 1-800-872-3838
(Site for asking business questions. Also has a business license
wizard. For $4, you can purchase *A Guide To Doing Business
In Maine And Business Start-Up Kit.*)

Maine Small Business Development Center
http://www.mainesbdc.org

Maryland

Maryland State Website
http://www.choosemaryland.org
(Follow the link to "Business Assistance" and to "Starting A
Business.")

Maryland Business Licensing Information
http://www.blis.state.md.us
Telephone: State License Bureau: 410-260-6240
(Site says not all businesses need a license. Call the above
number or contact your local Cerk of the Court to learn if you
need a license.)

Department of Labor, Licensing and Regulation (Professional Licenses)
http://www.dllr.state.md.us

Maryland State Department of Assessments and Taxation
http://www.dat.state.md.us
Telephone: 888-246-5941
Telephone: 410-767-1340 (Trade Name Search and Registration)

Massachusetts

Massachusetts State Site
http://www.mass.gov
(Follow the link to "Business Assistance" and to "Massachusetts Business Resource Team." Has a step-by-step guide to starting a business in Massachusetts.)
Telephone: 1-877-BIZ-TEAM   (1-877-249-8326)

Massachusetts Small Business Development Center (SBDC)
http://msbdc.som.umass.edu

Massachusetts Secretary of State
http://www.sec.state.ma.us
(In Massachusetts a DBA or certificate of assumed name is called a "Business Certificate" and is filed with the township.)

Massachusetts Department of Revenue
http://www.dor.state.ma.us
(Click on business information. Offers free Small Business Workshops. These state workshops tend to be excellent.)

http://www.dor.state.ma.us/business/licpermit.htm
(Licensing information. Contact the township or city which licenses local businesses.)

Michigan

Michigan Economic Development Corporation
http://medc.michigan.org
(Offers a complete guide to starting a business in Michigan. Information about licensing and name registration. DBAs are filed with the county clerk. The site has a link to the county clerks.)

Michigan Department of the Treasury
http://www.michigan.gov/treasury
(Follow the business link to "New Business" then to "Establishing a New Business." It has an Online Business Startup Wizard to help you determine what tax forms you need for your new business.)

Business Licensing Information
http://www.michigan.gov/statelicensesearch
(Not all businesses require licenses. Click on the link, "View ALL Required Licenses.")

Minnesota

Minnesota BizLinks
http://www.bizlinks.state.mn.us
(Links to business licensing and regulatory information.)

Minnesota Small Business Assistance Office
http://www.mnsbao.com

Minnesota Secretary of State
http://www.sos.state.mn.us
(Assumed name registration.)

Minnesota Department of Revenue
http://www.taxes.state.mn.us
Telephone: 651-297-8011

Minnesota Business Tax Education Partnership
http://www.uimn.org/tax/irs.htm
deed.tax@state.mn.us
(Free business tax workshops.)

The Department of Employment and Economic Development
http://www.deed.state.mn.us
(DEED publishes a free book *A Guide to Starting a Business in Minnesota*. To order a copy, call 651-296-3871. Outside the metro area, call 800-657-3858 or visit their website.)

Mississippi

Mississippi Home Page
http://www.mississippi.gov
(Click on "Business in Mississippi" and then go to "Home Based And Micro Businesses In Mississippi," which has specific information about starting a home-based business in Mississippi.)

http://msucares.com/business_assistance/homebusiness/index.html

Mississippi State University
http://msucares.com

Mississippi Development Authority
http://www.mississippi.org
(Click on "Business Development" and then go to "How to start a business." Mississippi Development Authority publishes the free book *The Entrepreneur's Tool Kit*.)
E-mail: eibus@mississippi.org
Telephone: Mississippi Development Authority:
601-359-3593

Mississippi Secretary of State
http://www.sos.state.ms.us

Mississippi Tax Commission
http://www.mstc.state.ms.us

Mississippi Small Business Development Centers (MSBDC)
www.olemiss.edu/depts/mssbdc

Missouri

Department of Economic Development
http://www.ded.mo.gov/business/startabusiness/
(Publishes the free book *Starting a New Business in Missouri*.)

Missouri Business Center (University Of Missouri)
http://www.missouribusiness.net
Telephone: 1-888-751-2863
(Describe your business, and you'll receive an information package tailored to your type of business. The Business Center answers business questions and publishes a "nuts and bolts" booklet about operating a business in Missouri.)

Entrepreneurship education on the web (eWeb) from Saint Louis University.
http://eweb.slu.edu

Missouri Small Business Development Centers
http://www.mobdn.net

Montana

Business Montana
http://www.bizmt.com

Montana Department of Commerce
http://commerce.state.mt.us
(Has a licensing guide and information about name registration.)

Montana Secretary of State
http://sos.state.mt.us
Telephone: 406-444-3665 (name registration)

Nebraska

Nebraska Home Page
http://www.nebraska.gov/
(Follow "Business" to "Starting A Business.")

Nebraska Department of Economic Security
http://assist.neded.org
Telephone: 800-426-6505

Nebraska Department of Revenue
http://www.revenue.state.ne.us

Nebraska Business Development Center
http://nbdc.unomaha.edu
(Offers $15 workshops about starting a business in Nebraska.
See website for current schedule. Also has a free pdf book *Keys
for Successful Business Start-Up: A Guide To Starting A
Business In Nebraska* which covers licensing, registration, and
other topics.)
Telephone: 402-595-1158

Nevada

Nevada Home Page
http://www.nv.gov
(Go to "Doing Business In Nevada.")

Nevada Secretary of State
http://sos.state.nv.us
(Note: DBA registrations *aren't* filed with the Secretary of State,
but with the County Clerk.)

Nevada Taxes
http://tax.state.nv.us

Nevada Taxes (Licensing Information)
http://tax.state.nv.us/taxnew/documents/
Business_License.pdf
(Unlike many states, Nevada requires all businesses to register
for a State Business License and to register to pay use tax. Home
businesses which earn less than about $22,000 were exempt
from this licensing.)

New Hampshire

The New Hampshire Small Business Development Center
http://www.nhsbdc.org

New Hampshire Secretary of State (Assumed name
registration)
http://www.sos.nh.gov

New Hampshire Department of Revenue
http://www.state.nh.us/revenue

Economic and Labor Market Information Bureau
http://www.nhes.state.nh.us/elmi/licertreg.htm
(A pdf describing licensed professions.)

New Jersey

New Jersey Business Resources
http://www.state.nj.us/brstrtop.html

Business Licensing and Registration
http://www.state.nj.us/njbgs/bgsclientreg.htm
Telephone: 609-292-1730 (Questions about registering for
taxes.)

Small Business Workshops
http://www.state.nj.us/treasury/taxation/text/
smallbustxt.htm

Small Business Workshops
Telephone: 609-984-4101
Taxpayer Services Branch
PO Box 269
Trenton, NJ 08695-0269

Business Formation and Registration
http://www.state.nj.us/treasury/revenue/busform1.htm
(Sole proprietors file name registrations with the county.)

New Mexico

New Mexico Regulation and Licensing Department
(professional licenses)
http://www.rld.state.nm.us

New Mexico Taxes
http://www.state.nm.us/tax/

Santa Fe Community College Small Business Development
Center
http://www.nmsbdc.org

New York

New York SBDC
http://www.nyssbdc.org

License and Permit Information
http://www.dos.state.ny.us/lcns/licensing.html
http://www.gorr.state.ny.us/gorr/
Governor's Office of Regulatory Reform
Telephone: 1-800-342-3464 (or 518-474-8275)

http://www.nylovessmallbusiness.com/
(You can order a "Start-Up Pack" of information online. Note:
Certificates of assumed name are called "Business Certificates"
in NY and are obtained from county clerks.)

Business Taxpayer Site
http://www.tax.state.ny.us/sbc/

North Carolina

North Carolina Commerce
http://www.nccommerce.com/servicenter/blio/startup/
(A good place to start for information about names, licenses,
etc. A certificate of assumed name is filed with the Register of
Deeds in the county of the business.)

Business License Information Office
http://www.nccommerce.com/servicenter/blio/
Telephone: 919 715-2864 or 1-800-228-8443

North Carolina Department of Revenue
http://www.dor.state.nc.us

North Carolina Secretary of State
http://www.secstate.state.nc.us/

The North Carolina Small Business and Technology
Development Center
http://www.sbtdc.org/

North Dakota

North Dakota Home Page
http://discovernd.com/business/
North Dakota Secretary of State
http://www.state.nd.us/sec/businessserv/registrations/
index.html
Register your DBA with the Secretary of State.

http://www.state.nd.us/businessreg/
New business registration.

State Tax Commissioner Site
http://www.state.nd.us/taxdpt/

Ohio

Ohio Business Portal
http://business.ohio.gov/

Ohio First-Stop Business Connection
http://www.odod.state.oh.us/onestop/index.cfm
Telephone: 1-800-248-4040 or 614-466-4232
(Call to order a free business information kit. Or e-mail:
1ststop@odod.state.oh.us)

http://business.ohio.gov/business_cycle/starting/
licenses_permits.shtml
(Information about licenses and permits.)

Ohio Small Business Development Center
http://www.odod.state.oh.us/edd/osb/sbdc/

Oklahoma

Oklahoma State Page
http://www.youroklahoma.com/
(Click on "Business." Then go to "Starting A Business.")

Oklahoma Tax
http://www.oktax.state.ok.us/oktax/busreg.html
Telephone: 405-521-3160
(Free business tax workshops.)

Oklahoma Secretary of State
http://www.sos.state.ok.us/
(Business Services.)

Oregon

Oregon Home Page
http://www.oregon.gov

Department of Economic and Community Development
http://www.econ.state.or.us/
(See "Small Business.")

Business Information Center
http://www.filinginoregon.com/
Telephone: 503-986-2200
(Business Information Packages about business licensing and
registration.)

Oregon Small Business Development Center Network
http://www.bizcenter.org/
541-463-5250

Oregon Business Guide From Secretary of State
http://www.filinginoregon.com/obg/toc.htm
(Assumed name registrations are filed with the Business
Registry.)

Pennsylvania

Pennsylvania Open For Business
http://www.paopen4business.state.pa.us
(See forms and publications.)

Pennsylvania Department of State
http://www.dos.state.pa.us
Telephone: 717-787-1057
(Sole proprietors register fictitious names with Secretary of State, Corporations Bureau.)

Department of Community and Economic Development
http://www.inventpa.com
(Click on "Business In PA." Offers a 134-page *Entrepreneur's Guide: Starting and Growing A Business In Pennsylvania*.)

Department of Revenue (See Business Taxpayers.)
http://www.revenue.state.pa.us/

Rhode Island

Rhode Island State Page
http://www.info.state.ri.us

http://www.tax.state.ri.us/
(Go to fast start business center for business licensing information. First, sole proprietors must register with your local city/town clerk's office. No state entity monitors sole proprietorships. To check your proposed business name against corporation names, trademarks, and service marks, call the Corporations Division at 401-222-3040.)

South Carolina

South Carolina Home Page (Click on "Business.")
http://www.myscgov.com

http://www.sctax.org/Publications/startbusns.html
(Publication: *A General Tax Guide for Starting a Small
Business in South Carolina.* You don't need to register sole
proprietorship businesses with the Secretary of State, but you
may need a local license.)

SC Business One-Stop Business Portal
http://www.myscgov.com/SCSGPortal/static/
scbos_00_tem2.html
(This is an ugly link, but I wanted to include it for you. Links to
licensing information. Probably an easier way to find the SC
Business One-Stop is just to search google.com for "South
Carolina Business One Stop." This site also offers complete
information guides for some popular businesses. For example,
there is a complete description of licensing and registration of
Child Day Care Services.)

SC Taxation
http://www.sctax.org/Tax+Workshops/default.htm
(Free tax workshops and a small business tax workshop manual
in pdf.)

South Dakota

South Dakota Home Page
http://www.state.sd.us/

http://www.state.sd.us/drr2/newbusiness.htm
New business information.

South Dakota Governor's Office of Economic Development
South Dakota Home Page
http://www.sdgreatprofits.com/
(A horrible web address which makes it look like a get-rich quick
site!)

http://www.sdgreatprofits.com/start-up/startup.htm
(Business start-up package.)

Business Start-Up Package
http://www.sdgreatprofits.com/start-up/step8.htm
Telephone: 800-872-6190 or 605-773-3301
E-mail: goedinfo@state.sd.us
http://www.sdgreatprofits.com/start-up/step8.htm
(Business licensing information.)

South Dakota Secretary of State
http://www.sdsos.gov/
(Fictitious name registration.)

Tennessee

Tennessee Business Services
http://www.state.tn.us/sos/bus_svc/

TN Department of Economic & Community Development
http://www.state.tn.us/ecd/res_guide.htm
(Small Business Information Guide. Sole proprietorships only
need approval from their city or municipality.)

TN Dept. of Revenue: Starting a New Business
http://www.state.tn.us/revenue/new_bus.htm

Texas

Texas Home Page
http://www.state.tx.us/
(Click on business and consumer services.)

Texas Department of Economic Development
http://www.tded.state.tx.us/guide/
Telephone: 1-800-888-0511
Online Book: *Starting a Business--4 Steps To Starting a Business*. Includes licensing information. Assumed name certificates are filed with your local county clerk.

Texas Small Business Advisor
http://www.cpa.state.tx.us/tba/

Utah

Utah Business Portal
http://www.Business.Utah.gov
(One-stop online business registration.)

Utah Department of Commerce
http://www.commerce.utah.gov
(Assumed names are registered with the Utah Division of Corporations and Commercial Code.)

http://www.utah.gov/business/main/index
(The State of Utah's *Guide to Doing Business in Utah*.)

http://www.utah.gov/business/starting.html
The State of Utah provides step-by-step instructions on how to start a business and answers many questions about starting a business.

Utah State Tax Commission
http://tax.utah.gov/
(Click on business information. Offers a 56-page booklet *Doing Business in Utah, A Guide to Business Information*. Also has free tax workshops specifically for sole proprietors.)

Free Tax Training Workshops
http://tax.utah.gov/training/workshops.html
Telephone: 801-297-6203, 1-800-662-4335, ext. 6203
Fax: 801-297-6358

Vermont

Vermont State Site
http://www.thinkvermont.com
(Click on "Small Business.")

http://www.thinkvermont.com/start/HTMLVer/index.html
(ThinkVermont.com offers a small business toolkit. Under "Documents and Forms" are the pdf booklets *Guide To Doing Business in Vermont* and *Vermont Guide To Business Taxes*.)

http://www.thinkvermont.com/start/HTMLVer/permits.html
(Discusses specialty permits you may require, such as special permits for an athletic trainer or a real estate appraiser.)

http://www.vermont-towns.org
(This link shows town and city licensing and zoning links. Note: In Vermont, you must register your business with *both* the Secretary of State and with your Town Clerk.)

Vermont Secretary of State
http://www.sec.state.vt.us
Telephone: 802-828-2363

Virginia

Virginia Department of Business Assistance
http://www.dba.state.va.us

Virginia Business Information Center
http://www.dba.state.va.us/virginia/center/
Has a link to a step-by-step *Guide to Starting a Business in Virginia.*

Virginia Department of Professional and Occupational Regulation
http://www.dpor.virginia.gov
Telephone: 804-367-8500

Washington

Washington Department of Licensing
http://www.dol.wa.gov/
http://www.dol.wa.gov/mls/startbus.htm (FAQ)
(Click on "Business." Especially see the Business License Frequently Asked Questions. Their "Master Application" includes name registration and licensing. When you apply for a master application, you'll receive a small business information package.)

Washington Department of Revenue
http://dor.wa.gov
(Click on "Doing Business." Then go to "New Business Information." Offers a Business Tax Guide in pdf and also tax workshops.)

West Virginia

West Virginia Secretary of State
http://www.wvsos.com
(Click on "Start A New Business" and go to "Smart Steps to Starting a Business in West Virginia." Name registration and licensing are covered.)

http://www.wvsos.com/business/startup/
soleproppartnership.htm
(Information for sole proprietors. The site says you should register with the State Tax Department and get a business franchise certificate before you begin doing business.)

http://www.wvsos.com/business/licensing/
professionallicensing.htm
(Professional licensing. Also, the site says to contact your County and your City Clerk for their requirements.)

Wisconsin

Wisconsin State Home Page
http://www.wisconsin.gov
(Click on "Business" and then "Build Your Business." Has links to professional licensing. If you operate under an assumed name, you must file a "Registration of Firm Name" with your County Register of Deeds. Sole proprietors can also file a trade name with the Secretary of State to gain further name protection.)

Wisconsin Secretary of State
http://www.sos.state.wi.us
(Only necessary if you wish to further protect your trade name or trademark.)

Wisconsin Department of Revenue
http://www.dor.state.wi.us/
(Click on "Business.")

Wyoming

Wyoming Secretary of State
http://soswy.state.wy.us
(Site says sole proprietors don't need to register with the
Secretary of State. However, you can register your name as a
trade name there.)

Wyoming Department of Revenue
http://revenue.state.wy.us/

University of Wyoming SBDC
http://uwadmnweb.uwyo.edu/SBDC/

Canada

Canadian Business Service Centers
http://www.cbsc.org/

Board of Trade of Metropolitan Montreal
http://www.infoentrepreneurs.org/
(The site says its mandate is to provide free help to
entrepreneurs throughout Canada.)

Small Business Information Canada
http://sbinfocanada.about.com/
(This is an about.com site. Not an official government
resource.)

Business Research Questions:

1. What state agency (if any) do I need to contact to register my certificate of assumed name? Or, is a certificate of assumed name registered locally in my state?

2. What are the websites for my specific state, city, and county? What business information do they provide?

3. What state agency and local government agencies do I need to contact to obtain licenses and permits for my business? Is my type of business specially regulated or not?

4. What are the zoning rules that apply to my *specific* home business and to my *specific* location? Will zoning be an issue? If so, how will I deal with it?

5. What state agency collects business taxes? If I need to collect state sales tax, with which agency do I register? Does my state require estimated tax payments? Use tax payments?

6. Does my state provide a free, comprehensive guide about starting a business? If so, where can I order it? Does my state provide free classes or workshops about starting a business or about business taxes? If so, where can I register for these workshops?

7. What Small Business Development Centers are located near me? What free information can they provide about starting a business in my state?

Use google.com to search for information relevant to the specific type of business you plan to start. Learn about the industry. For example, what information is available about being an auctioneer or about starting an event planning business? What associations are available that can provide you with further information? What local business organizations exist that might be useful to you?

I hope this chapter has introduced you to the level of free help that your state and local governments can provide you and has encouraged you to use the Internet to research and learn about your specific type of business and about your state and local requirements. Just as importantly, now that you've finished this book, I hope it gives you a jumping off point to register and start your new company. I wish you happiness and success in your new business. Peter

Small Business Resources

Websites

Ahbbo.com (A Home-Based Business Online. Articles by Elena Fawkner about operating an online home business)

IdeaCafe.com (Small business website)

Onlinewbc.gov (Online Women's Business Center)

PowerHomeBiz.com (Website devoted to home businesses)

SBA.gov (The Small Business Administration)

ThinkingLike.com (My website about entrepreneurship)

Tulenko.com (Site of small business columnist Paul Tulenko)

Books

Home Business

The Complete Idiot's Guide to Starting a Home-Based Business by Barbara Weltman

Home-Based Business for Dummies by Paul Edwards, Sarah Edwards, and Peter Economy

Making a Living Without a Job: Winning Ways For Creating Work That You Love by Barbara Winter

Working From Home: Everything You Need to Know About Living and Working Under the Same Roof by Paul Edwards and Sarah Edwards

General Small Business Startup Advice

Business Start-Up Kit: Everything You Need To Know About Starting And Growing Your Own Business by Steven D. Strauss

The Girl's Guide To Starting Your Own Business: Candid Advice, Frank Talk, And True Stories For The Successful Entrepreneur by Caitlin Friedman and Kimberly Yorio

Six-Week Start-Up: A Step-By-Step Program for Starting Your Business, Making Money, and Achieving Your Goals! by Rhonda Abrams

Small Business For Dummies by Eric Tyson

Start Your Own Business: The Only Start-Up Book You'll Ever Need by Rieva Lesonsky

Steps to Small Business Start-Up: Everything You Need to Know to Turn Your Idea Into A Successful Business by Linda Pinson and Jerry Jinnett

Thinking Like An Entrepreneur: How To Make Intelligent Business Decisions That Will Lead To Success In Building And Growing Your Own Company by Peter Hupalo

You Need To Be A Little Bit Crazy: The Truth About Starting And Growing Your Business by Barry J. Moltz

What No One Ever Tells You About Starting Your Own Business: Real Life Start-Up Advice from 101 Successful Entrepreneurs by Jan Norman

Small Business Taxes, Accounting, and Recordkeeping

Home Business Tax Deductions: Keep What You Earn by Stephen Fishman

J.K. Lasser's Small Business Taxes: Your Complete Guide to a Better Bottom Line by Barbara Weltman

J.K. Lasser's Taxes Made Easy for Your Home-Based Business: The Ultimate Tax Handbook for Self-Employed Professionals, Consultants, and Freelancers by Gary W. Carter

Keeping The Books: Basic Record-Keeping and Accounting For The Small Business by Linda Pinson

Minding Her Own Business: The Self-Employed Woman's Guide To Taxes and Recordkeeping by Jan Zobel

Small Time Operator: How To Start Your Own Small Business, Keep Your Books, Pay Your Taxes, And Stay Out Of Trouble! by Bernard B. Kamoroff

Working for Yourself: Law and Taxes for Independent Contractors, Freelancers and Consultants by Stephen Fishman

Marketing And Promotion

Get More Business Right Now! Tools & Ammunition Designed To Fight Off The Alligators And Get The Business You Need by Paul Tulenko

Grassroots Marketing: Getting Noticed in a Noisy World by Shel Horowitz

Guerrilla Marketing: Secrets for Making Big Profits From Your Small Business by Jay Conrad Levinson

Marketing Management by Philip Kotler

Marketing Outrageously: How to Increase Your Revenue by Staggering Amounts by Jon Spoelstra

What Clients Love: A Field Guide to Growing Your Business by Harry Beckwith

Index

Printed in the United States
72403LV00006B/159